Polka Dot Girls

Designed. Original. Treasured.

By
Kristie Kerr & Paula Yarnes

Copyright 2011 Kristie Kerr and Paula Yarnes. All Rights Reserved.

No part of this book may be reproduced, transmitted, or utilized in any form or by any means, graphic, electronic or mechanical, including photocopying, recording, taping, or by any information storage or retrieval, without the permission in writing from the publisher. WITH THE EXCEPTION OF THE POLKA DOT PLUS WEEKLY CHALLENGES, TAKE HOME ACTIVITY SHEETS AND PARENT PARTNERS, WHICH MAY BE DUPLICATED FOR GROUP USE ONLY.

Unless otherwise indicated, all Scripture quotations are taken from the Holy Bible, New Living Translation, copyright © 1996, 2004, 2007 by Tyndale House Foundation. Used by permission of Tyndale House Publishers, Inc., Carol Stream, Illinois 60188. All rights reserved.

THE HOLY BIBLE, NEW INTERNATIONAL VERSION®, NIV® Copyright © 1973, 1978, 1984, 2011 by Biblica, Inc.™ Used by permission. All rights reserved worldwide.

Scripture taken from The Message. Copyright © 1993, 1994, 1995, 1996, 2000, 2001, 2002. Used by permission of NavPress Publishing Group.

Scripture taken from the Contemporary English Version © 1991, 1992, 1995 by American Bible Society, Used by Permission.

Scripture taken from the Common English Bible P.O. Box 801 201 Eighth Avenue South Nashville, TN 37202-0801

ISBN: 987-0-9840312-1-4

Printed in the United States of America

2nd Printing

Contents

How To Use This Book 1

What is Beautiful 3–26
   Large Group Lesson 3
   Polk Dot Talk
      Kindergarten – 1st Grade 9
      2nd – 3rd Grade 11
      4th – 5th Grade 13
   Polka Dot Projects 15
   Polka Dot Plus
      Weekly Challenge 19
      Parent Partner 20
      Take Home Activity Sheets
         Kindergarten – 1st Grade 21
         2nd – 3rd Grade 23
         4th – 5th Grade 25

True Reflection 27–52
   Large Group Lesson 27
   Polk Dot Talk
      Kindergarten – 1st Grade 35
      2nd – 3rd Grade 37
      4th – 5th Grade 39
   Polka Dot Project 41
   Polka Dot Plus
      Weekly Challenge 45
      Parent Partner 46
      Take Home Activity Sheets
         Kindergarten – 1st Grade 47
         2nd – 3rd Grade 49
         4th – 5th Grade 51

Whatever 53–78
   Large Group Lesson 53
   Polk Dot Talk
      Kindergarten – 1st Grade 61
      2nd – 3rd Grade 63
      4th – 5th Grade 65
   Polka Dot Project 67
   Polka Dot Plus
      Weekly Challenge 71
      Parent Partner 72
      Take Home Activity Sheets
         Kindergarten – 1st Grade 73
         2nd – 3rd Grade 75
         4th – 5th Grade 77

Free to Be Me 79–102
   Large Group Lesson 79
   Polk Dot Talk
      Kindergarten – 1st Grade 85
      2nd – 3rd Grade 87
      4th – 5th Grade 89
   Polka Dot Project 91
   Polka Dot Plus
      Weekly Challenge 93
      Parent Partner 94
      Take Home Activity Sheets
         Kindergarten – 1st Grade 95
         2nd – 3rd Grade 97
         4th – 5th Grade 99

Why Am I Here? 103–128
   Large Group Lesson 103
   Polk Dot Talk
      Kindergarten – 1st Grade 109
      2nd – 3rd Grade 111
      4th – 5th Grade 113
   Polka Dot Project 115
   Polka Dot Plus
      Weekly Challenge 117

Parent Partner 118
　　　Take Home Activity Sheets
　　　　　Kindergarten – 1st Grade 119
　　　　　2nd – 3rd Grade 121
　　　　　4th – 5th Grade 125

God Confidence. 129-152
　　Large Group Lesson 129
　　Polk Dot Talk
　　　Kindergarten – 1st Grade 137
　　　2nd – 3rd Grade. 139
　　　4th – 5th Grade 141
　　Polka Dot Project 143
　　Polka Dot Plus
　　　Weekly Challenge. 145
　　　Parent Partner 146
　　　Take Home Activity Sheets
　　　　　Kindergarten – 1st Grade 147
　　　　　2nd – 3rd Grade. 149
　　　　　4th – 5th Grade 151

So Much Stuff! 153-176
　　Large Group Lesson 153
　　Polk Dot Talk
　　　Kindergarten – 1st Grade 161
　　　2nd – 3rd Grade. 163
　　　4th – 5th Grade 165
　　Polka Dot Project 167
　　Polka Dot Plus
　　　Weekly Challenge 169
　　　Parent Partner 170
　　　Take Home Activity Sheets
　　　　　Kindergarten – 1st Grade 171
　　　　　2nd – 3rd Grade. 173
　　　　　4th – 5th Grade 175

Courage 177-202
　　Large Group Lesson 177
　　Polk Dot Talk
　　　Kindergarten – 1st Grade 185
　　　2nd – 3rd Grade 187
　　　4th – 5th Grade 189
　　Polka Dot Project 191
　　Polka Dot Plus
　　　Weekly Challenge. 195
　　　Parent Partner 196
　　　Take Home Activity Sheets
　　　　　Kindergarten – 1st Grade 197
　　　　　2nd – 3rd Grade. 199
　　　　　4th – 5th Grade 201

Polka Dot Party 203

Dedicated to the girls who inspire us:

Anja who does funny accents...

JoJo who defies all odds...

Catelyn who is a SURVIVOR...

Lucy who LOVES unconditionally...

Betty who LIGHTS UP THE ROOM...

Dottie who loves tutus AND fishing poles...

Meg who is so funny she could possibly be the next Lucille Ball...

Ling who is NOT AFRAID to speak her mind...

Natalie who can organize like nobody's business...

Jeorgia who has AMAZING COURAGE...

and Lily who is simply sweet!

You amaze us.

Go change the world.

How to Use this Book

It seems easy enough, right? Like you really shouldn't need a page just to tell you how to use this book. And yet, here we are. We are nothing if we're not efficient!

Ok. This resource was written as a tool for use in a large group, small group or even for your family to use. Obviously, your specific needs may vary according to the size and make up of your group, but we have hopefully provided you with enough options that you have plenty of… well, options.

Each chapter starts with a large group lesson. This is something that can be taught by one teacher or even a variety of leaders. These lessons are designed to appeal to all age groups – so bring all your girls together for this part of the night. There are stories and illustrations provided, but feel free to add in your own thoughts, insights and stories! The girls will love to hear about your own personal experiences and perspective.

Following the large group time, there are questions for small group discussion. These are broken down by age group (K-1, 2-3, and 4-5)– so this would be a great time to divide the girls into smaller groups with separate leaders so that the discussion can be tailored to fit their level of experience and understanding. (If you don't have enough leaders to do small groups, keep the girls together and alternate questions from the various age level discussion questions.) Close out your small group time with a time of prayer. Invite the girls to pray for each other and take turns praying out loud. Not only will you learn a lot about your girls during this time, their little hearts will be bonded together when they spend time praying for one another.

Then it's craft time! We've included lots of fun ideas for you to do as a group. Make sure you do adequate preparation depending on the age and skill level of your girl. Nothing is more frustrating than running out of time because you spent too much time cutting things out or waiting for glue to dry. (By the way… glue dries REALLY slow. Even slower when you want it to dry fast. Just our experience anyway….)

Lastly, we've included some pages to be photocopied and sent home. They include a weekly challenge for the girls, age appropriate activity sheets, and a parent partner. These are intended to give the girls some fun tools to work on throughout the week and to let the parents keep up with what their daughters are learning.

And the MOST important thing to remember is to MAKE IT WORK FOR YOU. Every group is unique and different, so feel free to add, subtract, edit, rewrite, and rework anything you find here. Find out what works and stick with it and don't be afraid to chuck the stuff that isn't working.

Our job is simple – but it couldn't be more important. We get the amazing privilege of teaching these sweet girls about Jesus. We pray the material gives you practical tools to do just that. But above and beyond all that, remember that your gift of time and interest in these girls' lives will impact them far greater than any lesson or illustration. You are literally demonstrating for them what it means to be a woman who loves Jesus. Be patient. Be loving. Be fun. Be there.

We wish you all the best as you teach your girls what it means to be a Polka Dot girl!

Who Am I?

week 1

What is Beautiful?

WHAT'S THE POINT?

GOD MADE YOU JUST THE WAY YOU ARE... AND YOU SHOULD BE YOU!

theme verse
For we are God's masterpiece.
Ephesians 2:10

related bible passage
Psalm 139

❁ Large Group Lesson ❁

Being a girl is pretty awesome. It's so fun to be a girl – no matter what kind of girl you are! How many of you are "girly girls" who love dresses and anything super girly? How many of you are athletic girls who love to play sports? How many of you love school and reading books? How many of you love being outdoors and love animals? How many of you are a crazy combination of all of those things?!?

It's so cool how God made us all girls – and yet He made us all so different. We are the same in a whole lot of ways, but we are different in a whole lot of ways too!

The Bible tells us that God made each one of us.

*For you **created** my inmost being; you knit me together in my mother's womb.*
Psalm 139:12-14

Each and EVERY THING about YOU was HAND PICKED by God.

How many of you have gone to Build A Bear or Forever Friend workshop? It's a store where you can go and make your very own teddy bear or doll. The store has every size, color, style and outfit you can possibly imagine. And YOU get to go pick out every single thing about what you want your doll or bear to be like. Every combination is different – because it is hand picked by the person who is creating it!

And it was the same way when God created you! He picked out every single detail about you. He picked the color of your hair and the size of your ears. He decided what sports you would love or what instrument you would play with great skill. He determined the things you would be good at, and the stuff you would love to spend time doing. There is *Nothing* about you that wasn't hand picked by God when He created you!

And the Bible tells us that God was SO happy when He made you! He had created a lot of things – but creating YOU was the best thing He had ever done.

 *For we are God's masterpiece. He has created us anew in Christ Jesus, so we can do the good things he planned for us long ago.*
Ephesians 2:10

He only made ONE you. There is NO one with the amazing combination of looks, personality and talents that you have. You are one of a kind. You are so very special.

Sometimes I wonder why God didn't just make us all the same. Have you every thought about that? Why didn't He just make one person and then make another one exactly the same, and then another one exactly the same?

But God didn't! He made each one of us unique and different. Turn to the person next to you and find three things about them that are different from you. (Give them a moment to do this)

Polka Dot Girls ❁ Who Am I?

week 1

The Bible tells us that God is **CREATIVE**! Actually, He is called The Creator! To be creative means to use lots of variety and imagination to make something really special. And that's exactly what God did when He made us. He used lots of uniqueness and differences to make us all so special and different.

ILLUSTRATION:
Box of Crayons

How many of you like to color?

(Hold up a box of crayons. Begin coloring on a large piece of paper with just one color)

How many of you like to use just one crayon when you're coloring a picture? I mean, it would be a lot easier. You wouldn't have to spend time trying to decide which color to use. And then all of your pictures would look the same. It would be very neat and orderly, right?!

I don't know about you, but when I color, I like to use *All* the colors!

(Begin coloring, using the different colors) I love to use the bright purple to make something look happy and I like to use pink to make things look pretty and then I like to use black to outline things and sometimes I even like to use plain old green to color grass or a tree.

When God made us, He used every color in the box. He didn't make us all orange. He didn't make us all purple. He didn't even make us all plain old green. He made us with an amazing, beautiful combination of colors. He didn't make just one girl and then duplicate her over and over again. He made you special and unique. You are a masterpiece!

(It might be fun here to use different colors in the box to make some stick figure girls while you're describing how God made each of us unique!)

So tell me this: WHY do we spend SO much time trying to LOOK and ACT and BE just like everybody else? We try to be just like the "cool" kids at school. Or we think we should be just like our big sister or brother. Or we try and look like the girls we see on TV or magazines. Sometimes we feel bad about ourselves because we're different.

Can I tell you a secret? It's a really big one. Ready?!?!

You ARE different.

Yup. No way of getting around it. You are different. You are not like everybody else. There is not a person on the planet that is like you.

Phew. Glad we got that cleared up!

Now, here's my question to you. We KNOW that God made us each different and unique, right?! So why should we feel bad about that? Why should we try and change something that God planned? Why should we feel like we should be something other than EXACTLY who God made us to be?

I know that other people can put a lot of pressure on us to be just like everyone else. Sometimes we feel like our differences make us stand out and we really just want to blend in. We can be teased or left out because of our uniqueness, and that can be really hard.

But you know what? If you will stop worrying about what other people want you to be, and simply accept who God made you to be, you will feel so much better! God doesn't EVER make mistakes. And He didn't make ANY mistakes when He made you.

When God created you, He was doing it for a reason. You see, God knows everything about you. And God knows everything you are ever going to do with your life. Psalm 139:16 says *"You saw me before I was born. Every day of my life was recorded in your book. Every moment was laid out before a single day had passed."*

God picked all the unique things about you because He knew what you would need in order to do all the things He wanted you to do with your life!

It's like, if you were going to a friend's house to sleep over, you would pack your bag and make sure you had everything you needed for the next day or two. You'd make sure you had pajamas and your toothbrush, clothes for the next day and even clean underwear!!! You would think about all the things that you would need and then pack them in your bag so that you would have it when you needed it.

God packed your bag perfectly. He gave you everything you would need for your entire life when He created you. There is NOTHING about you that was

week 1

an accident. You were carefully and purposefully created to do all the things God has planned for your entire life!

Maybe God's plan for your life will have you going to another country and caring for children who don't have moms or dads. So He gave you a desire to travel and made you curious about other nations. He made you like different kinds of food and not be afraid of big spiders. And He gave you awesome hair that looks good in a ponytail for those really hot seasons. See? Everything about you is a part of God's plan. **There are no accidents and there are no mistakes.**

So, how about this? How about instead of feeling bad about the things that make you different, you start asking God to show you *Why* He made you the way He did. I bet if you start focusing on the cool reasons why God made you the way you are, you will feel less and less bad about the things that make you stand out from other people. You will start to get excited about the things that make you unique because they are a part of the incredibly awesome and amazing things God has planned for your life!

Jessie wasn't very good at sports. Actually, she stunk. She dreaded gym time at school because she was always picked last for teams and felt silly. The boys would pick on her because she couldn't do a cartwheel. In the summer time, all the girls in her class would play soccer together and spend lots of time having fun at practices and games, but Jessie was left out because she wasn't good enough to play on their soccer teams. She always felt like she didn't fit in.

But oh, how she loved to draw!! She could spend hours with her sketch pad making up characters and putting colors and designs together. Drawing came so easy to her and whenever she got the chance to create a new picture, her heart would soar.

One day, the girls on the soccer team came to her. They wanted to design t-shirts for their team to help raise money for some out of state tournaments. They wanted to come up with a really cool idea. They asked Jessie if she could draw a picture that the girls could put on their shirts.

Jessie was SO excited. She came up with some fun ideas and showed the girls the next day. They loved it! They ended up using a few of her drawings to make sweatshirts and coffee mugs too!

This experience was HUGE for Jessie. She realized that it was okay if she wasn't good at soccer – because she was good at other things! She didn't need to be like everybody else – she just needed to be herself! God had made her good at art – and so she should work as hard as she could on that, and not worry about the things she WASN'T good at.

She still got picked last in gym class. The boys still teased her. But it didn't matter as much as it used to. She knew that God had given her a special gift, and so it didn't matter to her if she wasn't good at sports.

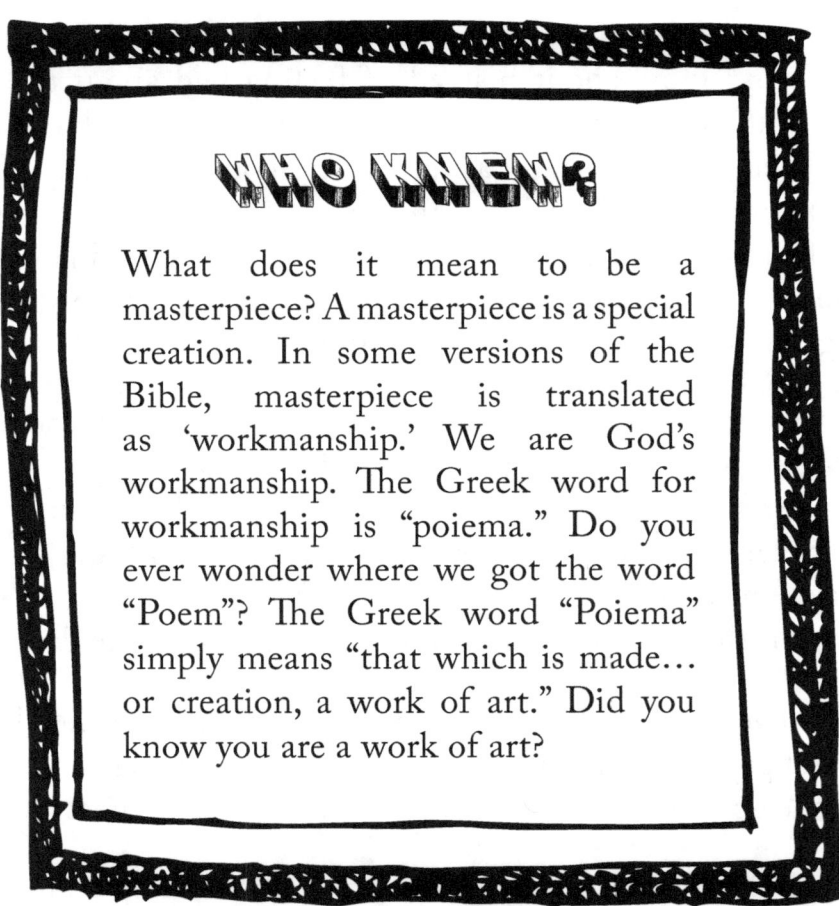

WHO KNEW?

What does it mean to be a masterpiece? A masterpiece is a special creation. In some versions of the Bible, masterpiece is translated as 'workmanship.' We are God's workmanship. The Greek word for workmanship is "poiema." Do you ever wonder where we got the word "Poem"? The Greek word "Poiema" simply means "that which is made… or creation, a work of art." Did you know you are a work of art?

You are unique. You are different. And you are EXACTLY who God created you to be.

Closing Prayer: Dear God. Thank you for creating me. I know that you made me unique and different for a purpose. I am so grateful that you hand picked

week 1

Kindergarten and 1st Grade Group Discussion Questions

1. Share with the group some things that you like to do or that you're good at. *(Let every girl have a minute or two to share)*

2. Share with the group something you don't like to do or maybe you're not very good at.

3. Notice that everyone in the group had different things that they liked to do! We all have things that we are good at, and we all have things that we're not so good at! Why do you think we're all so different?
    a. Because God made us that way!

4. What does it mean when we say that God "created" you?
    a. God picked out everything about you and made you before you were born.

5. What are some of the things God's picked out for you?
    a. Have each of the girls point out something unique about themselves.

week 1

2nd and 3rd Grade Group Discussion Questions

1. Share with the group some things that you like to do or that you're good at. *(Let every girl have a minute or two to share)*

2. Share with the group something you don't like to do or maybe you're not very good at.

3. Notice that everyone in the group had different things that they liked to do! We all have things that we are good at, and we all have things that we're not so good at! Why do you think we're all so different?
    a. Because God made us that way!

4. What does it mean when we say that God "created" you?
    a. God picked out everything about you and made you before you were born.

5. What are some of the things God's picked out for you?!
    a. Have each of the girls point out something unique about themselves.

Polka Dot Girls ❀ Who Am I?

week 1

4th and 5th Grade Group Discussion Questions

1. Share with the group some things that you like to do or that you're good at. *(Let every girl have a minute or two to share)*

2. Share with the group something you don't like to do or maybe you're not very good at.

3. Notice that everyone in the group had different things that they liked to do! We all have things that we are good at, and we all have things that we're not so good at! Why do you think we're all so different?
    a. Because God made us that way!

4. What does it mean when we say that God "created" you?
    a. God picked out everything about you and made you before you were born.

5. What are some of the things God's picked out for you?
    a. Have each of the girls point out something unique about themselves.

week 1

Older Girls Option

UNIQUE AS ME FLOWER PENS

Leaders Notes: Make sure you do adequate preparation for the crafts in accordance to the age and skill level of your group. For younger children, attach the fake flowers to the pen with floral tape prior to small group. The older girls may be able to attach the flower and decorate it in the allotted time frame.

Supplies Needed:
- Pens
- Silk Flowers with stem
- Green floral tape
- Scissors
- Small Self-adhesive jewels (optional)
- Glue
- Glitter
- Plastic bowl for glitter

Prep:
- Hold the flower next to the pen and clip the flower stem so it is about 2" up from the tip of the pen.
- Pour a small amount of glitter in a bowl for each group.

What should we do?
- Remove leaves.
- Make sure the flower sits on the top of the pen.
- While holding the flower stem tightly against the pen, wrap the entire length of the pen with floral tape. This will secure the pen and flower together.
- Decorate the petals of the flower.
  1. Small self-adhesive jewels (optional)
  2. Outline the petals with glue and dip in glitter for a finishing touch!

week 1

Younger Girl or All Girl Option

I'm God's Masterpiece Thumbprint Flowers

<u>Supplies Needed:</u>
- White Cardstock
- Different Colored Non-toxic Stamp Pads
- Markers and/or Crayons
- Thin-tipped Marker to outline flowers
- Small Self-adhesive Round Jewels (optional)
- Glitter Glue (optional)
- Hole Punch (optional)
- Pretty Ribbon (optional)

<u>Prep:</u>
- Make copies of the Flower Field template on white cardstock.
- Optional: Punch two holes at the top of the masterpiece.

<u>What should we do?</u>
- Have each girl pick out their favorite color ink for their flowers.
- On top of each blank stem have the girls create a flower with four index finger prints into an x shape.
- Color the rest of the masterpiece with markers/crayons.
- Optional: Outline the flowers with a thin tipped marker for a more dramatic result.
- Optional: Place a self-adhesive round jewel as the center of the flower.
- Optional: Use glitter glue to outline the flowers.
- Optional: Thread pretty ribbon through the pre-punched holes and tie at the top.

For WE are God's MASTERPIECE.
Ephesians 2:10

Polka Dot Plus

week 1

Weekly Challenge

Grow – GROW your faith by reading Psalm 139 this week. It talks about how God created everything about you!

Love – Think about a friend or family member. What are they good at? What are some of the ways in which God has created them uniquely? Once you have a few ideas, share them with that person. You will make their day!

Act – Spend some time working on an area that you feel like God has given you special abilities. Talk with your parents about getting some lessons, taking a class, for finding ways for you to use the unique gifts God has given you!

Memorize – MEMORIZE Ephesians 2:10: For we are God's masterpiece.

Parent Partner

Today we:

- 🌀 Talked about your daughter's uniqueness. God created her with such distinction and differences!

- 🌀 Learned that God hand picked everything about her before she was born. She was created uniquely and differently for a reason. God didn't make any two of us the same, He used His ultimate creativity to create each of us with our own distinct appearance, personality, gift set and temperament.

In a world that is pressuring our girls to fit into a certain mold and model, it is so important that we teach them to value the things that make them special. Help her realize that she is unique and different because God made **EACH ONE OF US** unique and different. Remind her that there are no two girls in the whole world that are exactly alike. When God made us, He used every color in the box!

Teach her to value her individuality. Help her develop the courage not to be just like everyone else. Be purposeful about helping her discover the unique talents and traits that God has given her and begin to provide opportunities for her to develop and use those gifts. For instance, if your child has a natural gift of compassion, give her opportunities to serve other people. Compliment her on her ability to make other people feel better. Provide times for her to use her compassion to help other people and make sure to point out that not everyone has the gift she has – that God specially designed her for this!

Polka Dot Girls ❀ Who Am I?

week 1

Kindergarten and 1st Grade Take Home Activity Sheet

I AM A MASTERPIECE!

My Name_____

My age _____

God made my eyes this color _____

God made my hair this color _____

My favorite sport _____

My favorite food _____

My special gifts God gave me (What am I good at)
_____
_____

When I grow up I want to be _____
_____

I love me because…. _____
_____

21

In the verses below, write in the word **YOU** in the blank spaces. (All scripture NIV)

_____ have searched me, LORD, and _____ know me. – Psalm 139:1

_____ know when I sit and when I rise; _____ perceive my thoughts from afar. – Psalm 139:2

_____ discern my going out and my lying down; _____ are familiar with all my ways. – Psalm 139:3

Before a word is on my tongue _____, LORD, know it completely. – Psalm 139:4

week 1

2nd and 3rd Grade Take Home Activity Sheet
I AM A MASTERPIECE!

My Name _____

My age _____

God made my eyes this color _____

God made my hair this color _____

My favorite sport _____

My favorite food _____

My special gifts God gave me (What am I good at)
_____
_____

When I grow up I want to be _____
_____

I love me because.... _____
_____

Each verse has a missing word that is identical. To discover that word, read each verse in your Bible and fill in the blanks. All scripture NIV

_____ have searched me, LORD, and _____ know me. – Psalm 139:1

_____ know when I sit and when I rise; _____ perceive my thoughts from afar. – Psalm 139:2

_____ discern my going out and my lying down; _____ are familiar with all my ways. – Psalm 139:3

Before a word is on my tongue _____, LORD, know it completely. – Psalm 139:4

For _____ created my inmost being; _____ knit me together in my mother's womb. – Psalm 139:13

I praise _____ I am fearfully and wonderfully made; your works are wonderful, I know that full well. – Psalm 139:14

My frame was not hidden from _____ I was made in the secret place, when I was woven together in the depths of the earth. – Psalm 139:15

_____r eyes saw my unformed body; all the days ordained for me were written in your book before one of them came to be. – Psalm 139:16

Polka Dot Girls ❀ Who Am I?

week 1

4th and 5th Grade Take Home Activity Sheet

Read Psalm 139:1-18 (NIV) and find the missing words in the Word Search puzzle.

¹You have _____ me, LORD, and you know me. ²You know when I sit and when I rise; you perceive my _____ from afar. ³You discern my going out and my lying down; you are _____ with all my ways. ⁴Before a word is on my tongue you, LORD, know it completely.

⁵ You _____ me in behind and before, and you lay your hand upon me.

⁶ Such knowledge is too _____ for me, too lofty for me to attain.

⁷ Where can I go from your _____ ? Where can I flee from your presence? ⁸ If I go up to the _____ , you are there; if I make my bed in the depths, you are there.

⁹ If I rise on the _____ of the dawn, if I settle on the far side of the sea, ¹⁰ even there your hand will _____ me, your right hand will hold me fast. ¹¹ If I say, "Surely the _____ will hide me and the light become night around me," ¹² even the darkness will not be dark to you; the night will shine like the day, for darkness is as _____ to you.

¹³ For you created my inmost being; you _____ me together in my mother's womb. ¹⁴ I praise you because I am fearfully and _____ made; your works are wonderful, I know that full well. ¹⁵ My frame was not hidden from you when I was made in the _____ place, when I was woven together in the depths of the earth. ¹⁶ Your eyes saw my unformed body; all the days ordained for me were _____ in your book before one of them came to be. ¹⁷ How _____ to me are your thoughts, God! How vast is the sum of them! ¹⁸ Were I to count them, they would outnumber the _____ sand— when I awake, I am still with you.

Word Search Puzzle

```
A C M L V W G R D Y R J C I W X
S E J I O P R E C I O U S Y K O
E I D G W N Y Q N Y K Y W K A A
C P V H R K L S L E N Z Q H T H
R Z Z T I W L C B G I O W F P V
E D V O T G U E Z D T X B Y Y I
T A J D T R F S N E V A E H L F
S O C A E A R A I L I M A F L W
E Y A G N I E X F W N D E Y Z S
A X T U U N D D U O C A I V R T
R M I I W S N W Y N J R D B T H
C T R D T D O D U K H K F I E G
H P I E W P W H H E H N P C X U
E Y P Q K L O R M F U E Z V L O
D O S E U O S G N I W S D L E H
A D J C T T Q S U M B S K L A T
```

Word List:

- searched
- thoughts
- familiar
- hem
- knowledge
- spirit
- heavens
- wings
- guide
- darkness
- light
- knit
- wonderfully
- secret
- written
- precious
- grains

Polka Dot Girls ❧ Who Am I?

Who Am I? — week 2

My True Reflection

What's the Point?
I need to see myself the way God sees me.

theme verse
How precious are your thoughts about me, O God.
Psalm 139:17 (NLT)

related bible verses
1 Corinthians 13:2

❋ Large Group Lesson ❋

When I was little, I used to practice singing in the mirror…with a hairbrush as my microphone. I would practice all my best rock star faces and best dance moves. I would have been **TOTALLY** embarrassed if anyone ever saw me – but I had to see what I looked like, right?!?

The mirror can be a good friend to you. One time I forgot to look in the mirror before I left the house in the morning, and later on in the day I realized that I had two different shoes on! Mirrors can save you from having something in your teeth, something in your nose and even something in your hair!

Mirrors are important. They show us what we look like. They show us what we need to fix. They are helpful when you're trying to look your best.

But, not all mirrors are helpful.

Good Girlfriend
Polka Dot Pointers

Have you ever had a friend with something in her teeth and you weren't sure if you should tell her or not? The answer is this: Friends tell friends! Wouldn't you want to know if YOU had something in YOUR teeth so you could fix it?! Find a quiet and non-embarrassing way to point out to your friend what she needs to fix – or even lean over and whisper in her ear.

Have you ever been to a fun house or a fair with a crazy mirror? The ones that make you look super tall or super skinny? Some of them make your head look really big and your legs look really short. Those mirrors are not giving you a true reflection of what you look like. (I sure HOPE I don't look like that!!!) The image you see looking back at you is misshapen and twisted.

And you know what? Sometimes you and I can start looking at ourselves in a "crazy mirror." Our view of ourselves can become crazy, misshaped and twisted. We can start to think things about ourselves that aren't true at all! When we look in the mirror we see someone who isn't pretty or talented or smart or funny, when the truth is that isn't who you are at all!! The refection you are seeing isn't real. It's **CRAZY!**

Polka Dot Girls ❁ Who Am I?

The Bible talks about seeing a reflection that isn't right. I Corinthians 13:12 says, *"Now we see things imperfectly as in a cloudy mirror, but then we will see everything with perfect clarity."* This scripture tells us that there are things right now that we think are true (about ourselves and even about God) that aren't accurate. They are a poor reflection that doesn't give us a clear picture.

Today we're going to talk about how important it is that you know your TRUE reflection. That you are looking in a mirror that is accurate. That you stop looking in a crazy mirror and instead look to God for a perfect reflection of who you are.

Let me ask you a question. What do you think about yourself? Do you think you're pretty? Do you think you're good at stuff? Do you think you're smart? What kinds of things do you say about yourself? Do you put yourself down a lot? Are you happy with who you are? Do you compare yourself to other girls and think that you're not as good as everyone else?

Sometimes we can be pretty hard on ourselves.

We can spend so much time thinking about all the things we're NOT, that we lose sight of who we ARE.

We focus on all the negative things, and pretty soon we don't really see ourselves the way we truly are. We see a distorted, crazy version of ourselves that isn't who we are at all!

> **ILLUSTRATION:** Invite a girl to come to the front. Have a bunch of objects for her to put on such as a wig, sunglasses, a large coat, high heel shoes or anything else you can think of.
>
> Imagine if my friend here looked in the mirror. What do you see?
>
> Ask these questions:
> - What color is your hair?
> - What color are your eyes?
> - How tall are you?
> - What color is your shirt?

Begin to put all the props on the girl.

Now ask the question:
- What color is your hair?
  (NOW it's HOT PINK – Or whatever color your wig is)
- Can you see what color your eyes are?
  (Can't tell – can't see my eyes anymore)
- How tall are you?
  (Well, I look two inches taller that I did before.)
- Can you see what color your shirt is?
  (I can't see my shirt anymore – I just see a big black coat.)

Polka Dot Girls ❀ Who Am I?

week 2

Okay. Is her hair REALLY pink now? NO! She was wearing a pink wig. It's not her REAL hair. What color are her eyes? They're still blue – even though we can't see them, right!? Did she really grow two inches taller? NO! She might seem taller because she has the big tall shoes on – but she's not REALLY taller. And what color is her shirt?! It's STILL red – even though the coat she put on makes it so we can't see her real shirt.

And some of you – are just like my friend here. You look in the mirror and you see a pink wig, sunglasses, tall shoes and a big coat. And you've just decided that is who you are. But it's NOT really who you are!!!! You've put on all these crazy things that make you look like something you are not! You have decided to believe a lot of things about yourself that aren't true and so you look in the mirror and see something that isn't really you at all!

Pretty soon, you don't even recognize yourself in the mirror anymore. You might think, "Well, I don't THINK I have pink hair, but everyone keeps telling me that I have pink hair… so I must have pink hair."

You've got to TAKE OFF all the extra stuff. You've got to stop believing the things other people say about you that aren't true. You have to stop thinking negative things about the way you look or the way you think or the things you aren't good at. Take off all the stuff that you've put on that makes your reflection look like someone who YOU ARE NOT!

Some of you have a really crazy view of yourself. You think a lot of things about yourself that aren't true at all. For whatever reason, you have picked up some things along the way and put them on and now the reflection you are seeing in the mirror isn't really you. It's not your true reflection.

So, what should we do? How do we get a real picture of who we are?

➡ 1. Stop picking on yourself

You know who can be the meanest person in the world to you? You. You know who can pick on you more than any other bully or mean girl? You. You know who can make you feel so bad about yourself you want to cry? You.

You and I can be so mean to ourselves! We tell ourselves that we're fat or ugly. We tell ourselves that we're not good at anything. We can be super critical of the things we do and say. We beat ourselves up because we aren't as good at something as other girls. We think negative things about the way we look, the way we think, and the things we do. We've got to STOP being so mean to ourselves! Imagine if another girl said all the things to you that you say to yourself? Would you still want to be friends with her? No way! Who would want to be around someone who was always putting us down and pointing out all the negative things about us?!

You need to be your own best friend! You need to be encouraging and kind to yourself. You may not be perfect, but there is no reason for you to beat yourself up all the time. When you catch yourself thinking something negative, STOP! 2 Corinthians 10:5 talks about controlling what we think about. The Bible tells us to take our thoughts captive which means we make sure we're not thinking things that aren't good and healthy for us. And saying negative things about yourself all the time is **NOT** good for you!

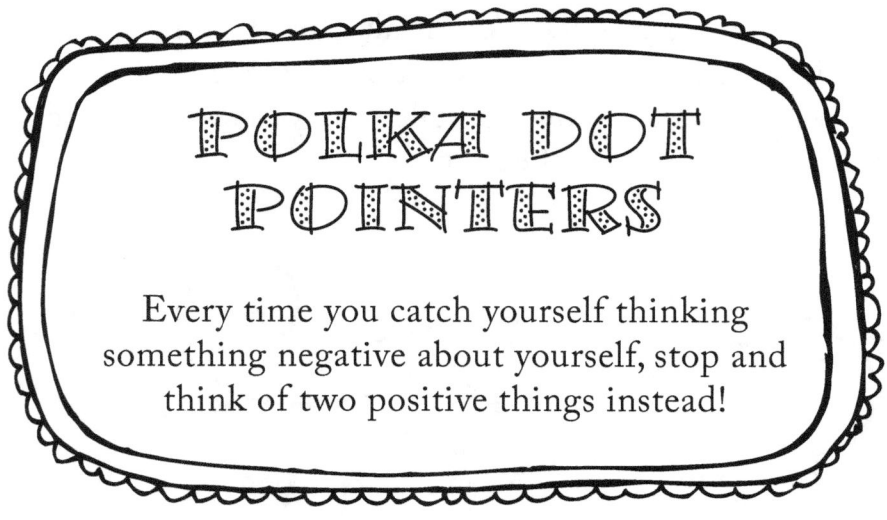

POLKA DOT POINTERS

Every time you catch yourself thinking something negative about yourself, stop and think of two positive things instead!

Stop focusing on your mistakes or the things you're not good at! Nobody's perfect and we all have things about us that we're working on. God loves you and doesn't want you picking on His favorite girl… **YOU!**

The best way to see your true reflection is to:

➡ 2. Know what GOD says about you.

Who is the person who knows you best? Is it your mom? Is it your best friend? Is it your sister? You might think that person knows everything about you, but you know what? God knows you better than ANYONE! He knows every thought you have and everything you have ever done or will ever do. God knows you best!

And He thinks you're pretty awesome!

God sees you perfectly. He created you and knows everything about you. His reflection of you is PERFECT. So instead of believing an idea about yourself that is cloudy and false, why not ask God to give you a REAL picture of who you are?

Ask Him to show you HIS view of you. Ask Him to remind you how He created you. When other people say things about you that aren't true, stop and listen instead to the voice of God. Ask God to show you the way He sees you. Ask Him to help you to hold on to HIS image of you and not the crazy picture of yourself that you see in your head.

You need to KNOW what God says about you! The most important voice in the whole wide world is the voice of God. His view of you is the true reflection of who you are. Everyone else's opinions, comments, and even your own view of yourself can be wrong. But God's view of you is perfect.

No one knows you like God does!

You need to keep asking Him to show you the way He sees you. When other voices start to play in your head – STOP and listen instead to the voice of God.

Do you know who HE says you are? He says you are His daughter. He says you are His friend – a GOOD friend. He says you are beautiful. He says you belong to Him. He says you can do anything because He will help you. He says you are gifted. He says you have a purpose. He says you are someone He wants to be around! He says you are His.

That's pretty cool, right! If the God of the Universe thinks all those things about you, why would you believe anything else! See yourself the way He sees you.

Closing Prayer: Dear God, Thank you that you see me as someone valuable. Forgive me for being so hard on myself. Help me to stop thinking bad things about who I am, and instead learn to see myself the way You see me. I love you. Amen.

week 2

Kindergarten and 1st Grade Group Discussion Questions

1. Have you ever seen a crazy fun house mirror at a carnival or a fair? What do you look like when you look into it? Is that what you really look like?

2. Why do you think that sometimes we think something about ourselves that isn't true?

    a. Sometimes people say mean things to us and so we think what they said is true.

    b. Sometimes we compare ourselves to other people and if we don't look like them, we feel bad.

    c. Sometimes we just get an idea in our heads about the way we look, or act, or think and we just keep thinking it even if it isn't true!

3. Can you think of something that you have thought about yourself that maybe wasn't true?

4. What are some ways you can stop thinking those things?

    a. Don't believe things other people say about you if it's not true.

    b. Don't keep thinking about something that isn't true.

    c. Think positive and nice things about yourself instead of thinking about the negative things.

5. Who knows you better than anyone else?

    a. Maybe mom, or friend or sister.

6. The truth is that GOD knows you better than anyone else! He knows everything about you! What do you think God thinks about you?

    a. He thinks I'm beautiful.

    b. He thinks I'm smart.

    c. He thinks I'm good at things.

Polka Dot Girls ❀ Who Am I?

week 2

2nd and 3rd Grade Group Discussion Questions

1. Have you ever seen a crazy fun house mirror at a carnival or a fair? What do you look like when you look into it? Is that what you really look like?

2. Why do you think that sometimes we think something about ourselves that isn't true?
    a. Sometimes people say mean things to us and so we think what they said is true.
    b. Sometimes we compare ourselves to other people and if we don't look like them, we feel bad.
    c. Sometimes we just get an idea in our heads about the way we look, or act, or think and we just keep thinking it even if it isn't true!

3. Can you think of something that you have thought about yourself that maybe wasn't true?

4. What are some ways you can stop thinking those things?
    a. Don't believe things other people say about you if it's not true.
    b. Don't keep thinking about something that isn't true.
    c. Think positive and nice things about yourself instead of thinking about the negative things.

5. Who knows you better than anyone else?
    a. Maybe mom, or friend or sister.

6. The truth is that GOD knows you better than anyone else! He knows everything about you! What do you think God thinks about you?
    a. He thinks I'm beautiful.
    b. He thinks I'm smart.
    c. He thinks I'm good at things.

Polka Dot Girls ❖ Who Am I?

week 2

4th and 5th Grade Group Discussion Questions

1. Have you ever seen a crazy fun house mirror at a carnival or a fair? What do you look like when you look into it? Is that what you really look like?

2. Why do you think that sometimes we think something about ourselves that isn't true?
   a. Sometimes people say mean things to us and so we think what they said is true
   b. Sometimes we compare ourselves to other people and if we don't look like them, we feel bad.
   c. Sometimes we just get an idea in our heads about the way we look, or act, or think and we just keep thinking it even if it isn't true!

3. Can you think of something that you have thought about yourself that maybe wasn't true?

4. What are some ways you can stop thinking those things?
   a. Don't believe things other people say about you if it's not true.
   b. Don't keep thinking about something that isn't true.
   c. Think positive and nice things about yourself instead of thinking about the negative things.

5. Who knows you better than anyone else?
   a. Maybe mom, or friend or sister.

6. The truth is that GOD knows you better than anyone else! He knows everything about you! What do you think God thinks about you?
   a. He thinks I'm beautiful.
   b. He thinks I'm smart.
   c. He thinks I'm good at things.

Polka Dot Girls ❀ Who Am I?

week 2

True Reflection Frame

Leaders Notes: Make sure you do adequate preparation for the crafts in accordance to the age and skill level of your group. For younger girls you may want to attach the list and ribbon to the frame prior to class. The older girls may be able to finish this project in the allotted time.

Supplies Needed:

- Cardstock (white or colored)
- Template of the list of things God says about His girls (two sizes available)
- Glue
- Foam or construction paper
- Pretty embellishments (foam stickers, flowers, jewels, glitter glue, etc.)
- Markers/crayons
- Hole punch (optional)
- Ribbon (optional)

Prep:

- Copy the desired template size onto cardstock.

What should we do?

- Glue the template onto foam or construction paper.
- Leave enough room around the edge of the cardstock and foam or construction paper to decorate with pretty embellishments.
- Punch two holes at the top of the foam or construction paper.
- Thread the pretty ribbon through the holes.
- Tie ribbon at the top into a bow.
- Hang on the wall!

I am God's daughter (John 1:12)

I am a FRIEND of Jesus (John 15:15)

I BELONG to God (1 Corinthians 6:20)

I have been chosen by God (Ephesians 1:3-8)

I have been FORGIVEN of all my sins (Colossians 1:13-14)

I am COMPLETE in Christ (Colossians 2:9-10)

I have direct access to God (Hebrews 4:14-16)

I am free from condemnation (Romans 8:1-2)

I CANNOT BE SEPARATED from the love of God (Romans 8:31-39)

I don't have to be afraid, because God has given me a spirit of power, love, and a sound mind. (2 Timothy 1:7)

I am the house that God lives in (1 Corinthians 3:16)

I am God's MASTERPIECE (Ephesians 2:10)

I can do all things thorough Christ who strengthens me (Philippians 4:13)

I am God's daughter (John 1:12)

I am a FRIEND of Jesus (John 15:15)

I BELONG to God (1 Corinthians 6:20)

I have been chosen by God (Ephesians 1:3-8)

I have been FORGIVEN of all my sins (Colossians 1:13-14)

I am COMPLETE in Christ (Colossians 2:9-10)

I have direct access to God (Hebrews 4:14-16)

I am free from condemnation (Romans 8:1-2)

I CANNOT BE SEPARATED from the love of God (Romans 8:31-39)

I don't have to be afraid, because God has given me a spirit of power, love, and a sound mind. (2 Timothy 1:7)

I am the house that God lives in (1 Corinthians 3:16)

I am God's MASTERPIECE (Ephesians 2:10)

I can do all things thorough Christ who strengthens me (Philippians 4:13)

Polka Dot Girls ❀ Who Am I?

Polka Dot Plus

week 2

Weekly Challenge

Grow: Grow by stopping any negative thoughts you have about yourself this week!

Love: Help a friend realize how God sees her by complimenting her on something this week.

Act: When you start thinking a negative thought about yourself, stop and say out loud TWO positive things instead!

Memorize: Psalm 139:17: *How precious are your thoughts about me, O God.* (NLT)

Parent Partner

So many girls struggle with negative thoughts about themselves. (Ah, who are we kidding… we ALL struggle with negative thoughts about ourselves!) Girls can really be hard on themselves when they don't think they measure up to others in their appearance, talents and personality. Little seeds of self doubt can grow and grow until the inner dialogue of self condemnation does significant damage to their beautiful little hearts.

This week we:

 Encouraged the girls to **STOP** picking on themselves and to see themselves the way God sees them. We want to help them learn to replace negative thoughts and ideas with the truth of God's word that says they are valuable, beautiful and gifted for purpose.

This week, encourage your daughter to open up about the things she struggles with in regards to her self-image. Help her work through the things she has begun to believe about herself and replace it with positive, life-giving messages. Below, you will see a list of scriptures we shared with the girls about who God says they are. Continue to discuss these with your daughter and spend some time praying that she would fully grasp how much God loves and values her. (and you too!)

- I am God's daughter (John 1:12)
- I am a friend of Jesus (John 15:15)
- I belong to God (1 Corinthians 6:20)
- I have been chosen by God (Ephesians 1:3-8)
- I have been forgiven of all my sins (Colossians 1:13-14)
- I am complete in Christ   (Colossians 2:9-10)
- I have direct access to God (Hebrews 4:14-16)
- I am free from condemnation (Romans 8:1-2)
- I cannot be separated from the love of God (Romans 8:31-39)
- I don't have to be afraid, because God has given me a spirit of power, love, and a sound mind. (2 Timothy 1:7)
- I am the house that God lives in (1 Corinthians 3:16)
- I am God's masterpiece (Ephesians 2:10)
- I can do all things thorough Christ who strengthens me (Philippians 4:13)

Polka Dot Girls ❖ Who Am I?

week 2

Kindergarten and 1st Grade Take Home Activity Sheet

Missing alphabet...write down the missing letter in the alphabet to find out the verse!

A B C D E F G I J K L M N O P Q R S T U V W X Y Z _____

A B C D E F G H I J K L M N P Q R S T U V W X Y Z _____

A B C D E F G H I J K L M N O P Q R S T U V X Y Z _____

A B C D E F G H I J K L M N O Q R S T U V W X Y Z _____

A B C D E F G H I J K L M N O P Q S T U V W X Y Z _____

A B C D F G H I J K L M N O P Q R S T U V W X Y Z _____

A B D E F G H I J K L M N O P Q R S T U V W X Y Z _____

A B C D E F G H I J K L M N O P Q R S T U V W X Y Z _____

A B C D E F G H I J K L M N O P Q R S T U V W X Y Z _____

A B C D E F G H I J K L M N O P Q R S T V W X Y Z _____

A B C D E F G H I J K L M N O P Q R T U V W X Y Z _____

A B C D E F G H I J K L M N O P Q R S U V W X Y Z _____

A B C D E F G H I J K L M N O P Q R S T U V W X Y Z _____

A B C D E F G H I J K L N O P Q R S T U V W X Y Z _____

A B C D F G H I J K L M N O P Q R S T U V W X Y Z _____

B C D E F G H I J K L M N O P Q R S T U V W X Y Z   _____

A B C D E F G H I J K L M N O P Q S T U V W X Y Z   _____

A B C D F G H I J K L M N O P Q R S T U V W X Y Z   _____

A B C D E F G H I J K L M N O P Q R S T U V W X Z   _____

A B C D E F G H I J K L M N P Q R S T U V W X Y Z   _____

A B C D E F G H I J K L M N O P Q R S T V W X Y Z   _____

A B C D E F G H I J K L M N O P Q S T U V W X Y Z   _____

A B C D E F G H I J K L M N O P Q R S U V W X Y Z   _____

A B C D E F G I J K L M N O P Q R S T U V W X Y Z   _____

A B C D E F G H I J K L M N P Q R S T U V W X Y Z   _____

A B C D E F G H I J K L M N O P Q R S T V W X Y Z   _____

A B C D E F H I J K L M N O P Q R S T U V W X Y Z   _____

A B C D E F G I J K L M N O P Q R S T U V W X Y Z   _____

A B C D E F G H I J K L M N O P Q R S U V W X Y Z   _____

A B C D E F G H I J K L M N O P Q R T U V W X Y Z   _____

A B C D E F H I J K L M N O P Q R S T U V W X Y Z   _____

A B C D E F G H I J K L M N P Q R S T U V W X Y Z   _____

A B C E F G H I J K L M N O P Q R S T U V W X Y Z   _____!

– Psalm 139:17 NIV

Polka Dot Girls ❀ Who Am I?

week 2

2nd and 3rd Grade Take Home Activity Sheet

A word is hidden in each line of letters. Find each word and write it on the lines below to figure out the verse. Once you discover the verse go to the Bible and read the entire chapter.

```
A B B C W H O W D O Y L T S M G V O X Y Z A I
M D O P R E C I O U S G M S U G I M E S T U V
G L J K B T O A Q S H I X Z W D E O R V A A C
N Y Z O A J L H G E X W Y B D F M E D L A S P
W U N D A R E S G L T A E F B E R M L M N O J
A P Z A P L A R O A N Y O B Y O U R K G E O R
U V D S P T H O U G H T S J K L M D D T Q E F
X Z Y M E G O D I Y M N A B O U T F O I J K Z
P R B A J G H P S A L M Q R T Z Y J K C F H I
```

_____ _____ _____   _____ _____ _____ _____
Line 1   Line 2

_____ _____ _____ _____ _____ _____ _____
Line 3   Line 4   Line 5   Line 6

_____ _____ _____ _____ _____ _____ _____ _____ _____!
           Line 7   Line 8

_____ _____ _____ _____ _____ 139:17
Line 9

WORD HELP:

Psalm   your   thoughts   to   God

precious   me   are   how

week 2

4th and 5th Grade Take Home Activity Sheet

TRUE REFLECTIONS CROSSWORD PUZZLE

To solve the puzzle, go to the Bible and read each scripture verse to find the answer to each crossword clue. A word list is attached if you need help. All scripture NIV.

Across

2. *For we are God's handiwork, X in Christ Jesus to do good works, which God prepared in advance for us to do.* – Ephesians 2:10

3. *...Instead, I have called you X, for everything that I learned from my Father I have made known to you.* – John 15:15

7. *For he has rescued us from the dominion of darkness and brought us into the kingdom of the Son he loves, in whom we have redemption, the X of sins.* – Colossians 1:13-14

10. *I can do all this through him who gives me X.* – Philippians 4:13

11. *Don't you know that you yourselves are God's X and that God's Spirit dwells in your midst?* – 1 Corinthians 3:16

Down

1. *Therefore, there is now no condemnation for those who are in Christ Jesus, 2 because through Christ Jesus the law of the Spirit who gives life has set you X from the law of sin and death.* – Romans 8:1-2

2. *Yet to all who did receive him, to those who believed in his name, he gave the right to become X of God.* – John 1:12

4. *For the Spirit God gave us does not make us timid, but gives us X, love and self-discipline.* – 2 Timothy 1:7

5. *...you were X at a price. Therefore honor God with your bodies.* – 1 Corinthians 6:20

6. *Let us then approach God's throne of grace with confidence, so that we may receive X and find grace to help us in our time of need.* – Hebrews 4:16

7. *...and in Christ you have been brought to X. He is the head over every power and authority.* – Colossians 2:10

8. *For I am convinced that neither death nor life, neither angels nor demons, neither the present nor the future, nor any powers, neither height nor depth, nor anything else in all creation, will be able to X us from the love of God that is in Christ Jesus our Lord.* – Romans 8:38-39

9. *For he X us in him before the creation of the world to be holy and blameless in his sight.* – Ephesians 1:4

Word List

fullness	*bought*	*created*	*forgiveness*	*mercy*
friends	*strength*	*chose*	*temple*	
power	*children*	*free*	*separate*	

Polka Dot Girls ❧ Who Am I?

Whatever!

WHAT'S THE POINT?
YOU DON'T HAVE TO BELIEVE THE THINGS OTHER PEOPLE SAY ABOUT YOU.

theme verse
If God is for us, who can ever be against us?
Romans 8:31

related bible story
Mark 5:28-34

❀ Large Group Lesson ❀

Kaitlyn didn't know what to think. She had moved to a new school over the summer and now she found herself in a totally new place where everything was different. At her old school, she knew everyone and had lots of friends. But things couldn't have been more different now.

For some reason, a couple of the popular girls decided that they did *Not* like her. They refused to let her sit at their table at lunch. They whispered behind her back at recess. And worst of all, they started saying things about her that were untrue.

They said that she had cheated on her homework. They said that she thought she was better than everyone else. And worst of all, they started saying bad things about her family.

Kaitlyn was so upset! How could people that she barely knew seem to have it in for her?! Why would someone say such horrible things about her? She had never, ever cheated before! She didn't think she was better than everyone – she was a good friend! And the things that were said about her family were just plain old lies.

The hardest part about all of it is that Kaitlyn started to believe the rumors herself. At first she was angry, but as time went on she was just hurt and the more hurt she got, the more she started to think that maybe those people were right about her. Maybe she wasn't a very nice girl. Maybe she wasn't a very good friend. Maybe her family wasn't the greatest. In her heart she knew these things weren't true, but sometimes when you hear things enough, you can start to wonder if maybe they are true.

Have you ever had anyone say anything "not so nice" about you?

It can be really easy to believe what other people say about you. You can have all kinds of unkind things said about you; about how smart you are or how popular you are (or aren't), whether or not you're good at something and even if you're a good friend.

I don't know why people can be so mean to each other. I wish it didn't happen. But the truth is, sometimes people are just mean. They say things that hurt our feelings and make us feel bad about ourselves.

There are **LOTS** of stories in the Bible of girls who had to overcome what other people said about them. There was Esther, who had people hate her because of her family and where she came from. There was Leah, who the Bible says was "unloved." There was a woman in the New Testament who was sick and so other people treated her really meanly and if she came near them, they would get really upset.

These girls had to let God help them work through these things. God helped Esther be brave and stand up to the person who was coming after her family. God blessed Leah with lots of children because He saw that she was being treated poorly. And Jesus healed the woman with the disease and showed her love and compassion when other people left her out.

Polka Dot Girls ❁ Who Am I?

week 3

And God will help you to work through the times when you face people being mean to you and saying things about you that make you feel bad. The Holy Spirit will comfort you, and He will help you know what to do in those situations.

So, what do you do when someone says something about you that hurts your feelings or makes you feel bad about yourself?

The first thing you need to do is:

➡ 1. Let go of the hurtful things people say about us.

When someone says something about you that hurts your feelings, or makes you feel like you're not good at something, it's easy to keep thinking about it over and over again. You replay those words or actions in your mind and continue to feel bad about it.

But instead of holding onto those unkind words, why don't you try just letting them go? Every time you start to think about it, stop yourself and say, "No way! I'm not going to think about that anymore!"

My kids love to get balloons filled with helium at our favorite restaurant. My daughter Dottie loves to get balloons, but sometimes she lets go of it on our way to the car and the balloon goes flying way up into the sky. What if, when someone says or does something to you that hurts your feelings, you imagine that you put all those unkind words or thoughts into a balloon and let it go up into the sky and fly right up to Jesus! Instead of holding onto to it, and replaying it in your mind, just let it go instead. Send up all those hurtful things and let Him take them out of your heart and mind. I promise it will help you feel better!

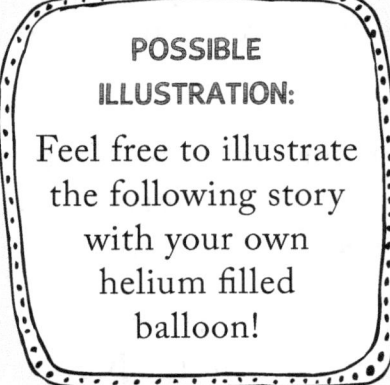

POSSIBLE ILLUSTRATION:

Feel free to illustrate the following story with your own helium filled balloon!

Jesus is the VERY best at helping you through something that has hurt your heart. If you keep bringing those thing things to Him, He will help you feel better.

A while ago, I hurt my finger. I had a really big cut on my hand and man oh man did it hurt. The only thing that would make it feel better is if I took a bandage and wrapped it really, really tight around the cut. If I took the bandage off, it would start to hurt again. So I would put on another really tight bandage to help it feel better.

There is a verse in the Bible that says that God will be like a big bandage to your heart when your feelings are hurt. Song of Solomon 8:6 says, *"Place me like a seal over your heart."* When you are feeling badly about something that someone has said or done to you, run to Jesus and let Him wrap Himself around your heart like a big bandage. He will help your heart get better and He will help it not hurt as much too. He loves you and wants to help you work through the hard stuff we go through sometimes.

So, let go of the things that people say and let Jesus help your heart feel better.

The second thing you need to do when someone says or does something that hurts your feeling is:

➡ 2. Forgive the people that hurt you.

Some of you have had really hurtful things said to you. You have been teased. Someone has told you that they don't want to be your friend anymore. It can be so hard to understand why people would hurt you and make you feel bad. Sometimes it just doesn't make sense and the LAST thing you want to do is forgive someone who has made you feel so bad.

But the Bible says that we are supposed to FORGIVE the people that hurt us. Colossians 3:13 says, *"Make allowance for each other's faults, and forgive anyone who offends you. Remember, the Lord forgave you, so you must forgive others."*

This is NOT an easy thing to do, is it?! We don't want to forgive them, we want to get back at them! We want them to feel bad for hurting us. But the Bible says that we are supposed forgive them! We are to let go of the desire to get back and get even and to trust that God will take care of us. Proverbs 20:22 says, *"Don't say, 'I will get even for this wrong. Wait for the LORD to handle the matter.'"*

week 3

As much as you want to hold onto your anger and hurt, and as much as you want to see the person who has hurt you feel bad, Jesus says that you have to forgive them. To forgive someone is to stop being mad at them and not to hope that something bad will happen to them. On our own, it is really, really hard to forgive someone. But Jesus will help you to forgive the people who have hurt you.

And the last thing you should do when someone says or does something to you that hurts you is:

⇨ 3. Learn to say "you're not my mudder!"

You're probably wondering, "What in the world does that mean?!?" I'll tell you!

When my daughter Betty was about four years old, she loved to boss her older brother Charlie around. Charlie was seven years old at the time and his little sister definitely knew how to get him upset.

Her favorite thing to do was to tell him that he had to turn off his video games. She would march up in front of the television set and say, "Charlie! You have to turn off your games RIGHT NOW or you are going to be grounded." She would put her hand on her hip and shake her finger in his face and make sure he knew that she was NOT happy with him.

Charlie would come running to me so upset saying, "Betty says that I have to turn off my video games! I just got started!" I would assure him that he DIDN'T have to turn off his games yet, but he would just look at me so sad and say, "But Betty says I have to."

Finally, I had enough. I said to Charlie, "Betty is NOT your mother. I am your mother. Just because she *Acts* like she is the boss of you and THINKS she is the boss of you DOESN'T make her the boss of you. She is not your mother and you do not have to do what she says." He seemed to understand what I was saying to him and a little while later I heard Betty trying to boss him around again. Charlie looked her right in the eye and said, "You're not my mudder!"

A few weeks later, I was dealing with someone who had said something about me that hurt my feelings. They said something that wasn't true and I was starting to believe what they had said. I mean, they sure acted pretty sure of themselves – maybe they were right. Suddenly, I said out loud, "You know what? You're not my mudder!"

Just because someone acts like they know everything about you doesn't mean they really know you. Just cause someone says that you act a certain way doesn't make it true. Just because someone acts like the boss of you, doesn't mean they are.

I have learned that when people say things about me I have to stop myself and ask "Is what they're saying about me true?" If it's not, then I say, "You're not my mudder!" I refuse to believe something that someone says to me that isn't true or kind. Instead of believing the lie or sitting quietly by and letting them talk about you, don't be afraid to look them right in the eye and say, "Whatever! You don't know what you're talking about."

Learn to say to yourself, "They may act like they know what they're talking about, but I KNOW who I am and I refuse to believe what they are saying about me." You don't have to believe the things that other people say about you. You have to know what God says about you and believe the truth of who you are.

You have to KNOW who you are. Not what other people SAY you are. Not what other people THINK you are. Not what other people WANT you to be. But WHO YOU ARE.

WHO are you? You are valuable. You have something to offer the world. You are worth knowing. God made you – for a purpose and He has plans for your life. God is for you. He believes in you and thinks you are AMAZING. Romans 8:31 says, *"If God is for us, who can ever be against us?"* It doesn't matter what anyone else says about you, because you know that God knows you best and loves you most.

Some of you have been really hurt by the things other people have said to you. God wants to help you let go of those things and let Him heal the hurt in your heart. He wants to help you forgive the people that have said or done mean things to you.

Polka Dot Girls ❀ Who Am I?

week 3

Some of you have allowed yourselves to believe what other people have said about you. You are feeling bad about what you look like or what your abilities are or even what your family is like because of the things people have said. Today, Jesus wants to give you the strength and courage to say "You're not my mudder!" to the people who are trying to hurt you and instead stand confidently in who God created you to be. He wants you to stand proudly as the daughter who He made you to be. You don't have to believe what other people say about you.

Closing prayer: Dear God, I have been hurt by the things other people have said about me. Help me to let go of those things and not to believe the lies. Please heal my heart and help me forgive the people who have hurt me. And give me the strength to stand up and not believe the lies that are said about me. I love you. Amen.

Polka Dot Girls ❀ Who Am I?

week 3

Kindergarten and 1st Grade Group Discussion Questions

1. Have you ever had someone say something about you that wasn't true? How did that make you feel?

2. What should you do with those hurt feelings and negative things that were said about you?

    a. Give them to Jesus.

    b. Send them up to heaven just like they were in a balloon.

3. Is there something in your heart that you need Jesus to heal? Share it with the group if you feel comfortable.

4. What does it mean to forgive someone?

    a. To not want to get them back.

    b. Stop wanting to see bad things happen to them.

    c. To let go of the thing they said or did that hurt you.

5. What should you say when someone says something about you that is untrue?

    a. "Whatever! You don't know what you're talking about!"

    b. "You're not my mudder!"

    c. See if the girls can come up with any other ideas.

6. Say the theme verse together a few times:
    "If God is for us, who can ever be against us?" – Romans 8:31

7. What should you do if you find yourself starting to believe the things other people say about you?

    a. Remind yourself of who you really are!

    b. Refuse to believe things about yourself that aren't true.

    c. Remember who God says you are!

week 3

2nd and 3rd Grade Group Discussion Questions

1. Have you ever had someone say something about you that wasn't true? How did that make you feel?

2. What should you do with those hurt feelings and negative things that were said about you?
    a. Give them to Jesus.
    b. Send them up to heaven just like they were in a balloon.

3. Is there something in your heart that you need Jesus to heal? Share it with the group if you feel comfortable.

4. What does it mean to forgive someone?
    a. To not want to get them back.
    b. Stop wanting to see bad things happen to them.
    c. To let go of the thing they said or did that hurt you.

5. What should you say when someone says something about you that is untrue?
    a. "Whatever! You don't know what you're talking about!"
    b. "You're not my mudder!"
    c. See if the girls can come up with any other ideas.

6. Say the theme verse together a few times:
   "*If God is for us, who can ever be against us?*" – Romans 8:31

7. What should you do if you find yourself starting to believe the things other people say about you?
    a. Remind yourself of who you really are!
    b. Refuse to believe things about yourself that aren't true.
    c. Remember who God says you are!

Polka Dot Girls ❀ Who Am I?

week 3

4th and 5th Grade Group Discussion Questions

1. Have you ever had someone say something about you that wasn't true? How did that make you feel?

2. What should you do with those hurt feelings and negative things that were said about you?
   a. Give them to Jesus.
   b. Send them up to heaven just like they were in a balloon.

3. Is there something in your heart that you need Jesus to heal? Share it with the group if you feel comfortable.

4. What does it mean to forgive someone?
   a. To not want to get them back.
   b. Stop wanting to see bad things happen to them.
   c. To let go of the thing they said or did that hurt you.

5. What should you say when someone says something about you that is untrue?
   a. "Whatever! You don't know what you're talking about!"
   b. "You're not my mudder!"
   c. See if the girls can come up with any other ideas.

6. Say the theme verse together a few times:
   "*If God is for us, who can ever be against us?*" – Romans 8:31

7. What should you do if you find yourself starting to believe the things other people say about you?
   a. Remind yourself of who you really are!
   b. Refuse to believe things about yourself that aren't true.
   c. Remember who God says you are!

Polka Dot Girls ❦ Who Am I?

week 3

My "Whatever" Thoughts Pail

Supplies Needed:
- Colored cardstock
- White or colored paper
- White pails with handles (Oriental Trading has them in units of 12)
- Styrofoam cups can be used as a less expensive alternative.
- Ribbon, different colors and styles
- Pretty embellishments (self-adhesive foam shapes, jewels, flowers, etc.)
- Permanent markers
- "Whatever" scripture copied on pretty paper.
- Copy of the word "Whatever"

Prep:
- Copy the "Whatever" template on colored cardstock. Cut the cardstock template so each girl has the word "Whatever"
- Copy "Whatever" scriptures on white or colored paper (one sheet per girl)
- Cut ribbon into 6" pieces. Cut enough ribbon so that each girl will have at least four 6" pieces to adorn her pail.

What should we do?
- Glue or stick the word "Whatever" on the front of the pail.
- Give each girl a copy of the "Whatever" scriptures to cut out. Fancy scrapbooking scissors are fun to use!
- Decorate the pail with pretty embellishments and/or markers.
- Tie many pieces of pretty ribbon around the handle
- Put the cut out "Whatever" scriptures in the pail.

Explain to the girls that when they need encouragement they can pull a scripture out of their "Whatever" pail. Replacing earthly thoughts with God thoughts!

Whatever	Whatever	Whatever
Whatever	Whatever	Whatever
Whatever	Whatever	Whatever
Whatever	Whatever	Whatever
Whatever	Whatever	Whatever
Whatever	Whatever	Whatever
Whatever	Whatever	Whatever
Whatever	Whatever	Whatever
Whatever	Whatever	Whatever
Whatever	Whatever	Whatever

"Whatever" Scripture

If God is for us, who can ever be against us? – Romans 8:31

You are altogether beautiful, my darling, beautiful in every way. – Song of Solomon 4:7

And yet, O LORD, you are our Father. We are the clay, and you are the potter. We all are formed by your hand. – Isaiah 64:8

Make allowance for each other's faults, and forgive anyone who offends you. Remember, the Lord forgave you, so you must forgive others. – Colossians 3:13

Don't say, "I will get even for this wrong. Wait for the LORD to handle the matter. – Proverbs 20:22

For I know the plans I have for you," says the LORD. "They are plans for good and not for disaster, to give you a future and a hope. – Jeremiah 29:11

Place me like a seal over your heart... – Solomon 8:6

I am leaving you with a gift – peace of mind and heart. And the peace I give is a gift the world cannot give. So don't be troubled or afraid. – John 14:27

Obviously, I'm not trying to win the approval of people, but of God. If pleasing people were my goal, I would not be Christ's servant. – Galations 1:10

Don't be concerned about the outward beauty of fancy hairstyles, expensive jewelry, or beautiful clothes. You should clothe yourselves instead with the beauty that comes from within, the unfading beauty of a gentle and quiet spirit, which is so precious to God. – 1 Peter 3:3-4

But the LORD said to Samuel, "Don't judge by his appearance or height, for I have rejected him. The LORD doesn't see things the way you see them. People judge by outward appearance, but the LORD looks at the heart. – 1 Samuel 16:7

Finally, brothers and sisters, whatever is true, whatever is noble, whatever is right, whatever is pure, whatever is lovely, whatever is admirable – if anything is excellent or praiseworthy – think about such things. – Philippians 4:8

Polka Dot Girls ❧ Who Am I?

Polka Dot Plus

week 3

Weekly Challenge

Grow: Grow your faith be reading the story of Esther in the Bible and see how she courageously overcame the negative things other people said about her and her family.

Love: If you see someone being picked on, stand up for them! Maybe they don't know what to do… but you do! Say, "Whatever! You don't know what you're talking about!"

Act: Write down some things that you have believed about yourself that are untrue. Then cross it out and write out the **TRUTH** of who you are instead!

Memorize: Romans 8:31 *"If God is for us, who can ever be against us."*

Parent Partner

Our girls are faced with criticism, teasing and other difficult situations each and every day. I know my first reaction is to simply go find the offending person and go all "mama bear" on them! But I have learned to restrain myself from beating up other people and instead try to equip my daughters with the tools to hear hurtful things and not let it grab hold of their hearts.

This week we:

- Taught your daughters to let go of the things that are said to them that hurt them. Not to replay them over and over in their minds, but instead to send them up to heaven just like a helium balloon. Jesus will help them work through the hurt that comes from those harsh words and heal the pain that they are feeling.

- Encouraged the girls to forgive the people who have hurt them. The Bible asks us to let go of the desire for revenge. We need to trust God to take care of the people who are hurting us, and forgive them instead. (You're gonna have to work on this too… I have a REALLY hard time forgiving people who hurt my babies. Gggrrrrrrrrrr……..)

- And lastly, we encouraged your girls to have some perspective when other people say and do things that hurt them. Just because someone says something about them, it doesn't make it true! They don't have to believe those lies and rumors. We encouraged them to say, "Whatever! You don't know what you're talking about" when someone says something untrue about them.

Continue to encourage your daughters to work through the things people say about them. Lead them by your example of forgiveness. And help them know who they are in Christ, regardless of what anyone else might say to them.

week 3

Kindergarten and 1st Grade
Take Home Activity Sheet

What should I do?

- Connect the dots to find out what the object is.
- When complete, draw a picture showing how your feelings have been hurt or how someone has made you feel not good enough.
- You can also write down some things that you have believed about yourself that are untrue.
- Color the object.

Now…pray to God to help you let go of those thoughts and forgive those people who have hurt you. Let it GO and give it to God!

week 3

2nd and 3rd Grade
Take Home Activity Sheet

What should I do?

- Connect the dots to find out what the object is.
- Write down some things that you have believed about yourself that are untrue.
- Color the object.

Now…pray to God to help you let go of those thoughts and forgive those people who have hurt you. Let it GO and give it to God!

Search the Chart

	A	B	C	D	E	F
1	What	the	us	and	response	care
2	to	against	now	above	you	don't
3	have	who	don't	ever	then	believe
4	about	say	things	can	is	be
5	for	shall	Romans	name	know	If
6	trust	we	so	in	these	God

Find the words on the chart and write words below to discover the verse. Check your answer by reading Romans 8:31 NIV.

| _____ | _____ | _____ | _____ | _____ |
| A/1 | E/3 | B/5 | B/6 | B/4 |

| _____ | _____ | _____ | _____ | _____? |
| D/6 | E/1 | A/2 | E/6 | C/4 |

| _____ | _____ | _____ | _____ | _____, |
| F/5 | F/6 | E/4 | A/5 | C/1 |

| _____ | _____ | _____ | _____ | _____? |
| B/3 | D/4 | F/4 | B/2 | C/1 |

_____ 8:31 NIV
C/5

Polka Dot Girls ❀ Who Am I?

week 3

4th and 5th Grade
Take Home Activity Sheet

Write down some things in the balloon that you have believed about yourself that are untrue.

Now…pray to God to help you let go of those thoughts and forgive those people who have hurt you. Let it *GO* and give it to God!

Search the Chart

	A	B	C	D	E	F
1	What	the	us	and	response	care
2	to	against	now	above	you	don't
3	have	who	don't	ever	then	believe
4	about	say	things	can	is	be
5	for	shall	Romans	name	know	If
6	trust	we	so	in	these	God

Find the words on the chart and write words below to discover the verse. Check your answer by reading Romans 8:31 NIV.

_____ _____ _____ _____ _____
A/1   E/3   B/5   B/6   B/4

_____ _____ _____ _____ _____?
D/6   E/1   A/2   E/6   C/4

_____ _____ _____ _____ _____,
F/5   F/6   E/4   A/5   C/1

_____ _____ _____ _____ _____?
B/3   D/4   F/4   B/2   C/1

_____ 8:31 NIV
C/5

Polka Dot Girls ❀ Who Am I?

Who Am I?
week 4

Free to Be Me

WHAT'S THE POINT?

GOD MADE YOUR BODIES AND YOU ARE BEAUTIFUL JUST THE WAY YOU ARE.

theme verse

Dear friends, God is good. So I beg you to offer your bodies to Him as a living sacrifice, pure and pleasing. That's the most sensible way to serve God. Don't be like the people of this world, but let God change the way you think. Then you will know how to do everything that is good and pleasing to Him.

Romans 12:1-2

related bible verses

1 Corinthians 1:18-31

❋ Large Group Lesson ❋

If you could change one thing about the way you look, what would it be? Maybe you think you're too tall or too skinny. Maybe you think you're too short or your hair is too curly. Maybe you think your nose is too big or your ears are too small. Maybe you think your skin is the wrong color or your feet are the wrong size.

Most of us have SOMETHING about our bodies that we don't like. There are things about us that make us feel different. We don't look like the girls in the magazines or the girls in our schools. It's really easy to point out all the things about our physical appearance that we just wish were different!

There is a verse in the Bible that says this exact thing! Romans 9:20 says, *"Should what is formed say to him who formed it," Why did you make me like this?"* Have you ever asked God that question, "Why did you make me like this?" I sure have.

In this chapter, we are going to look at the way we view our appearance and how we can have a healthy perspective of our bodies and the unique way God made each and every one of us.

So, what is your body image? Basically, it is the way you feel about your appearance. It's how you view yourself. We get our body image from the things other people say to us, from the things we see in magazines and on TV, and the way we think we measure up to those images.

Maybe you've seen a picture of someone who you think is really pretty and now you struggle with feeling bad because you don't look the same as the picture. Maybe at school, everyone likes the girls who look a certain way, and because you don't look like that, you don't like yourself very much. Your body image, the way you see yourself, is shaped by what other people think (what you THINK other people THINK!).

But God wants you to have a GOOD body image. He made you unique and beautiful, and He doesn't want you feeling bad about the way you look!

So, how do we overcome a negative body image? How can you feel better about the way you look? What can you do to accept and love the body that God gave you? We're going to look at a scripture in the Bible that tells us three things that can help us be ok with the way we look.

Dear friends, God is good. So I beg you to offer your bodies to him as a living sacrifice, pure and pleasing. That's the most sensible way to serve God. Don't be like the people of this world, but let God change the way you think. Then you will know how to do everything that is good and pleasing to him. – Romans 12:1-2 CEV

The first thing we need to do to have a healthy body image is to:

➡ 1. Change the Way You Think.

week 4

Have you ever learned something one way, and then suddenly you had to learn a different way to do the same thing? My kids brought home some math homework and when I sat down to help them, it didn't take me long to realize that the teachers had taught them a different way to solve the problems than the way I learned it when I was in school. Every time I look at a problem, I automatically start thinking about it in a certain way and then I have to stop and make myself think about the NEW way to answer the question. It's not easy, because my mind tends to think a certain way! (And my kids like to tease me about it too!!)

If you have a certain way of thinking about things, it can be hard to stop thinking that way and change your thoughts. But that is EXACTLY what you need to do when it comes to your body image. You need to change how you think about the way you look. It can be so easy to simply think the worst about yourself. You can constantly put yourself down and look for the negative things about your body and appearance.

But instead of always thinking about the negative, what if you thought about the things you like! Instead of comparing yourself to other girls, what if you simply decided that it was okay to be you! The Bible says that God will help us feel peaceful about the way we look if we FIX our thoughts on Him and who He created us to be. Isaiah 26:3 says, *"You will keep in perfect peace all who trust in you, all whose thoughts are fixed on you."*

When you start to think something negative about yourself, just STOP yourself and then change your thoughts to something positive! When you begin to compare yourself to the girls on TV, fix your mind on the fact that God created you just the way He wanted you to be. Ask God to help you to change the way you think about your body and appearance. He will help you!

The second way we can do to have a healthy body image is

⇒ 2. Don't Be Like the People Of the World

Answer this for me: Who decides what's cool? Who decides what's popular? Who decides what's pretty and what's not pretty? It's kind of a silly question, isn't it? I don't really know the answer. I guess a lot of times we decide what is cool and pretty based on what we see on TV or magazines. But WHY? Why do the people who make the TV shows and magazines get to decide what is pretty and cool? Who are these people?!? And why do they get to decide whether or not I'm cool?! It's pretty silly if you ask me.

The Bible says we are to "*not be like the people of the world.*" This means that we're not supposed to strive to be what the world tells us is popular or beautiful. 1 Corinthians 1:28 tells us, "*What the world thinks is worthless, useless, and nothing at all is what God has used to destroy what the world considers important.*" Instead of focusing on what the world says is beautiful, we should focus on what God says is beautiful.

And what does God say is beautiful? Well, let's take a look around. God created us all so different from each other, didn't He?! If he wanted us to all look the same, He would have created us that way! But He didn't. He made us unique and a million different shades of beautiful.

FLOWER ILLUSTRATION: Have a number of varied fresh or silk flowers that show a wide variety of shapes and colors. Take a minute and show each flower individually and have the girls call out some of the distinct things of each flower (this one's orange, exotic, smells good… this one's red, is elegant, etc.)

I have a question for you. Which one of these flowers is pretty?

(Let the girls call out different answers.)

The answer is this: All of them. Each one is different, but beautiful in it's own way. They're not the same, but they are beautiful. God created so many different kinds of flowers because each and every one of them brings a certain kind of beauty to the world. I'm so glad that God didn't only create one kind of flower!

And you and I thinking that you have to look a certain way to be beautiful is just like us saying that the only flower that is pretty is a red rose. Yes, the red rose is beautiful, but it isn't the ONLY beautiful flower!

Polka Dot Girls ❀ Who Am I?

You may look different than your friends. You may look different than the girls on TV. But who says that means you aren't beautiful!?!? That's just silly.

We need to stop looking to the world to tell us what is beautiful. God has SHOWED us what is beautiful in the way He created us – unique and different. Let's stop thinking that we have to look like what the world says, and embrace God's view of creative beauty!

So, we should change the way we think, stop believing what the world says about beauty and lastly, we should:

⇨ 3. Offer your bodies to God as a living sacrifice.

I bet you're wondering what a sacrifice is?! In the Old Testament, people used to come to the Temple and bring a gift to give to God called a sacrifice. Now, they didn't just bring any old offering, they would select the very best animal or food that they had and give it to God to show Him that they loved Him. It was something they had taken good care of and gave willingly to God out of their devotion to Him.

So, what does it mean to offer our BODIES as a living sacrifice to God? It means that we need to tell God that our bodies belong to Him. We should take good care of them because we want to give Him the very best we have to offer. We want to give our bodies to God so we can do anything He may ask of us.

You see, God has a HUGE, GINORMOUS plan for your life. He has given you gifts and talents that are all housed inside this physical body He has given you. He wants you to use the things He has given you to accomplish all kinds of amazing things!

If you're not taking care of your body, then you can't give God your very best sacrifice. If you're putting it down all the time and hating things about your offering, then you're not bringing a very good sacrifice to God. If you're not honoring the body God gave you by making sure that you're not doing anything that can harm you, you're not bringing a very good sacrifice to God.

I don't know about you, but I want to give God the very best I have. I want to give Him a body that I am proud of, I want to give Him a body that is ready to do anything He may ask of me! I want to give Him the very best sacrifice I can.

So, instead of being negative and critical about the way you look, choose to think positive things about the way God made you! Refuse to buy into the world's way of thinking that says we all have to look alike. And take good care of the body God has given you so that you can do great things for God!

Closing Prayer: Dear God, I thank you for the body you gave me. I know that you made me special and unique. Help me to change the way I think about the way I look. I want to see things the way YOU see them, not the way the world sees them. I offer my body as a sacrifice for you, because I love you. Amen.

week 4

Kindergarten and 1st Grade Group Discussion Questions

1. What does "body image mean?"
   a. Your body image is the way you see yourself.
   b. It's what you think about how you look.

2. Why do you think it is so easy to find things we don't like about the way we look?
   a. Sometimes other people tease you about things.
   b. We look different from other people.

3. God wants you to feel GOOD about the way you look! He created you just the way you are! Today we discussed 3 things that will help us feel good about the way we look. Do you remember what they are?
   a. Change the way you think.
   b. Don't be like the people of the world.
   c. Offer your bodies to God as a living sacrifice.

4. How can you change the way you think about what you look like?
   a. Don't think bad things about the way you look.
   b. Don't talk badly about yourself.
   c. Don't try and look like everyone else.
   d. Be okay with being who God made you to be.

5. How can we think differently than the world does about beauty?
   a. Remember that God made us all different.
   b. There are lots of different kinds of beautiful – just like the flowers.
   c. If YOU were a flower, what kind of flower would you be?! Why?

6. How can you offer your body as a living sacrifice to God?
   a. By taking care of your body.
   b. By being proud of the body God gave you.
   c. By doing anything God asks you to do!

week 4

2nd and 3rd Grade Group Discussion Questions

1. What does "body image mean?"
   a. Your body image is the way you see yourself.
   b. It's what you think about how you look.

2. Why do you think it is so easy to find things we don't like about the way we look?
   a. Sometimes other people tease you about things.
   b. We look different from other people.
   c. We compare ourselves to other girls and feel bad if we don't look like them.

3. God wants you to feel GOOD about the way you look! He created you just the way you are! Today we discussed 3 things that will help us feel good about the way we look. Do you remember what they are?
   a. Change the way you think.
   b. Don't be like the people of the world.
   c. Offer your bodies to God as a living sacrifice.

4. How can you change the way you think about what you look like?
   a. Don't think bad things about the way you look.
   b. Don't talk badly about yourself.
   c. Don't try and look like everyone else.
   d. Be okay with being who God made you to be.

5. How can we think differently than the world does about beauty?
   a. Remember that God made us all different.
   b. There are lots of different kinds of beautiful – just like the flowers.
   c. If YOU were a flower, what kind of flower would you be?! Why?

6. How can you offer your body as a living sacrifice to God?
   a. By taking care of your body.
   b. By being proud of the body God gave you.
   c. By doing anything God asks you to do!

week 4

4th and 5th Grade Group Discussion Questions

1. What does "body image mean?"
   a. Your body image is the way you see yourself.
   b. It's what you think about how you look.

2. How do you feel about your body? Is your body image good or bad?

3. Why do you think it is so easy to find things we don't like about the way we look?
   a. Sometimes other people tease you about things.
   b. We look different from other people.
   c. We compare ourselves to other girls and feel bad if we don't look like them.

4. God wants you to feel GOOD about the way you look! He created you just the way you are! Today we discussed 3 things that will help us feel good about the way we look. Do you remember what they are?
   a. Change the way you think.
   b. Don't be like the people of the world.
   c. Offer your bodies to God as a living sacrifice.

5. How can you change the way you think about what you look like?
   a. Don't think bad things about the way you look.
   b. Don't talk badly about yourself.
   c. Don't try and look like everyone else.
   d. Be okay with being who God made you to be.
   e. Don't listen to the negative things other people say about you.

6. How can we think differently than the world does about beauty?

    a. Remember that God made us all different.

    b. Don't worry about what you see on TV or in magazines. Looking and dressing like those girls is NOT the only way to be beautiful.

7. If YOU were a flower, what kind of flower would you be!? Why?

8. How can you offer your body as a living sacrifice to God?

    a. By taking care of your body.

    b. By being proud of the body God gave you.

    c. By doing anything God asks you to do!

    d. By not doing things to harm your body.

    e. By not putting things into your body that could hurt it, like drugs or alcohol or smoking.

    f. By exercising and eating healthy.

week 4

"I Pick Me" Flower!

Leaders: Make sure you do adequate preparation for the crafts in accordance to the age and skill level of your group. For younger children, cut out the flower before class. Older children should be able to cut out the flower and decorate it in the allotted time.

Supplies Needed:
- Cardstock in different colors
- Flower template
- Large Tootsie Pops (one/girl)
- Pretty embellishments
- Markers/crayons
- Glue sticks
- Glitter
- Tape

Prep:
- Copy the flower template onto many different colors of cardstock.

What should we do?

- On each petal write something you LOVE about yourself.
- Decorate each petal with pretty embellishments, markers and/or crayons.
- Rub the glue stick on the flower where you would like to sprinkle a little glitter.
- Sprinkle glitter on your flower!
- Poke a small hole in the center of the flower.
- Slide the Tootsie Pop stick through the hole in the center of the flower to create a pretty center to your flower and a stem.
- Tape the bottom to secure.

Polka Dot Plus

week 4

Weekly Challenge

Grow: Grow your faith by reading **1 Corinthians 1:18-31**. It talks about how God's view is so different from the world's view!

Love: This week is all about loving YOU. Spend some time thinking about the things you LIKE about the way you look!

Act: Anytime you find yourself comparing the way you look to another girl, stop and find 2 things about yourself that you like. Write them down and remind yourself that you are uniquely beautiful!

Memorize: Romans 12:1-2 *¹Dear friends, God is good. So I beg you to offer your bodies to him as a living sacrifice, pure and pleasing. That's the most sensible way to serve God. ²Don't be like the people of this world, but let God change the way you think. Then you will know how to do everything that is good and pleasing to him.*

Parent Partner

If there was one thing I could GUARANTEE for my daughters, I would wish that they would never struggle with their body image. Our girls face so much pressure to fit into a tiny little mold of what the world says is beautiful, and many of them endure a lifelong struggle with a negative body image.

The most important thing you can do for them is to lovingly affirm their beauty. I know it's easy for us to want to spare them from teasing and comparisons by trying to help them "fit the mold" better – but how much more could we serve them by shattering the mold altogether.

God created us uniquely beautiful. He made a variety of shapes, sizes and colors because it PLEASED Him to do so. So when we begin to define beauty in the narrow terms that the world tells us, not only do we set ourselves up for a lifetime of struggle, we dishonor the creativity of our Creator.

Encourage your daughter to see the beauty in diversity. Show her that she is created differently by design. When she is trying to squeeze herself into the tiny little box of the world's definition of beauty, blast it wide open with the truth of who God made her to be.

Our theme verse for the week is Romans 12:1-2 which says, *"Dear friends, God is good. So I beg you to offer your bodies to him as a living sacrifice, pure and pleasing. That's the most sensible way to serve God. Don't be like the people of this world, but let God change the way you think. Then you will know how to do everything that is good and pleasing to him."*

Encourage your daughter to do just that. Change the way they think about their bodies. Stop the negative thoughts towards the way they look. Don't be like the people of the world, defining beauty in narrow terms. And offer your bodies as a living sacrifice to God. Offering the best you possibly can by taking care of your body and honoring it.

week 4

Kindergarten and 1st Grade Take Home Activity Sheet

The pictures below are symbols of words that will help you understand how God wants you to view your body.

Ask your Mom or Dad to help you figure out the missing words by cutting out the symbol and placing it in the correct sentence to complete the special message from God.

Dear _____,
God is good.

That's the most sensible way to _____ God.

So I beg you to offer your _____ to him as a living sacrifice, pure and pleasing.

Don't be like the people of this _____, but let God change the way you think.

Then you will know how to do everything that is good and pleasing to him.
– Romans 12:1-2 CEV

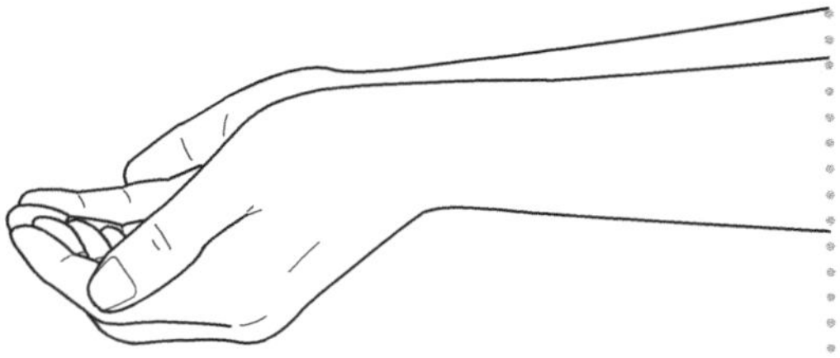

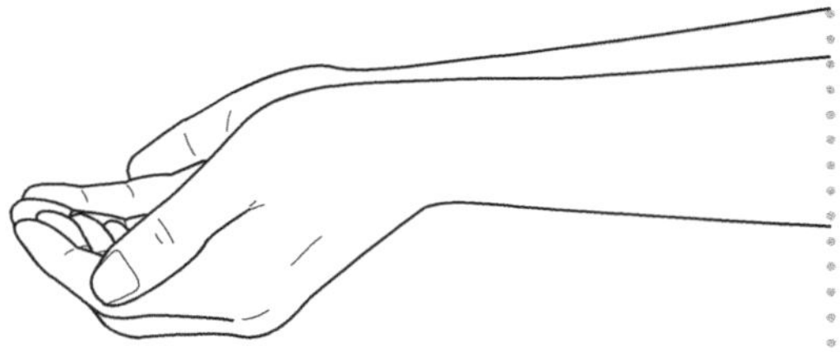

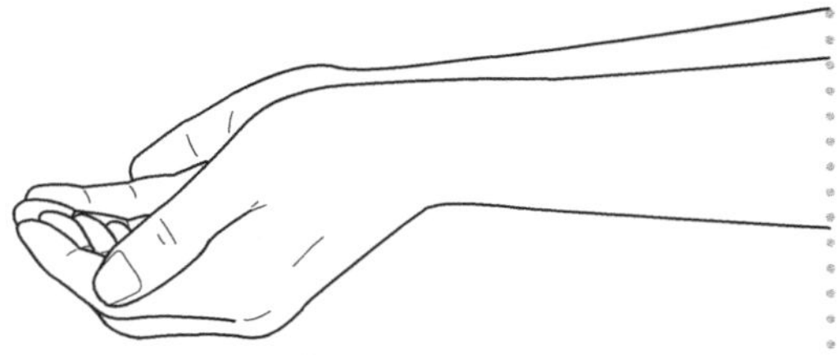

week 4

2nd and 3rd Grade Take Home Activity Sheet

Unscramble the following words and put them into the blanks in the verse below. Try to do it without looking at the word list!

Step 1: Unscramble the words.

stsirse   __ __ __ __ __ __ __

ycerm   __ __ __ __ __

biosed   __ __ __ __ __ __

fscaeciri   __ __ __ __ __ __ __ __ __

lodrw   __ __ __ __ __

eagcdnh   __ __ __ __ __ __ __

ttes   __ __ __ __

doog   __ __ __ __

Step 2: Put the words into the correct verse.

¹Brothers and _____,

God has shown you his _____.

So I am asking you to offer up your _____ to him while you are still alive.

Your bodies are a holy _____ that is pleasing to God. When you offer your bodies to God, you are worshiping him.

2 Don't live any longer the way this _____ lives.

Let your way of thinking be completely _____.

Then you will be able to _____ what God wants for you.

And you will agree that what he wants is right. His plan is _____ and pleasing and perfect.

– Romans 12:1-2 NIV

Word List

sisters	world	bodies
good	sacrifice	mercy
test	changed	

Polka Dot Girls ❖ Who Am I?

week 4

4th and 5th Grade Take Home Activity Sheet

Unscramble the following words, put the words into the correct verses. Go to the Bible, read Romans 12:1-2 NIV and write the verses in the correct order.

Step 1: Unscramble the words.

stsirse   __ __ __ __ __ __ __

ycerm   __ __ __ __ __

biosed   __ __ __ __ __ __

fscaeciri   __ __ __ __ __ __ __ __

lodrw   __ __ __ __ __

eagcdnh   __ __ __ __ __ __ __

ttes   __ __ __ __

doog   __ __ __ __

Step 2: Put the unscrambled words into the correct sentence.

So I am asking you to offer up your _____ to him while you are still alive.

Then you will be able to _____ what God wants for you.

Brothers and _____,

Your bodies are a holy _____ that is pleasing to God. When you offer your bodies to God, you are worshiping him.

Let your way of thinking be completely _____.

And you will agree that what he wants is right. His plan is _____ and pleasing and perfect.

Don't live any longer the way this _____ lives.

God has shown you his _____.

– Romans 12:1-2 NIV

Word List

sisters	changed	world
sacrifice	test	mercy
good	bodies	

Polka Dot Girls ❀ Who Am I?

Step 3: Write the verses in the correct order to reveal God's word to you!

Polka Dot Girls ❀ Who Am I?

Why Am I Here?

WHAT'S THE POINT?

GOD HAS A PURPOSE FOR YOUR LIFE.

theme verse

I know the plans I have in mind for you, declares the LORD; they are plans for peace, not disaster, to give you a future filled with hope.
Jeremiah 29:11 (CEB)

related bible story

Jeremiah 1:1-9

❁ Large Group Lesson ❁

Have you ever had a "To Do" list? Maybe your mom or dad has given you a list of things that you needed to get done before you could go outside and play. Maybe your teacher at school has given you a list of things you need to work on before lunch time. Or maybe you just like to make lists for yourself! I love to make lists and then cross them out when I finish what's on it. It's a really good feeling to cross things off a list!

Do you know that God has a "To Do" list for you? It's true! And it's not just a list for what you need to do today or tomorrow, He has a list of what He wants you to do EVERY DAY OF YOUR WHOLE ENTIRE LIFE! He has big plans for you! Jeremiah 29:11 says, *"I know the plans I have in mind for you, declares the LORD; they are plans for peace, not disaster, to give you a future filled with hope."* (CEB)

WHO KNEW?

Have you ever heard of a "To Do" list? It's a list of things you need to get done. Sometimes other people make a "To Do" list FOR you. And sometimes, your parents might call it a "Honey Do" list because it sounds nicer to say "Honey, could you please do this for me?!" But it still means the same thing, "Hey! Get this done!"

You know what I think is just amazing? That God lets you and I be a part of His plans. I mean, He's GOD! If He wanted something done, He could just say the word and He could make anything happen. (Kind of like He did when He created the whole universe!!!) But instead, He lets you and me be His helpers! He gives us jobs to do and then He gives us all the things we need to get the job done. I think that's pretty awesome.

God uses people to do His work on earth. He tells us in the Bible that we are to help take care of the people on earth. We're to help those who need help. We're to be kind and show the love of God to others. And most importantly, we are to tell other people about Jesus!

week 5

So, how do we know what is on our "To Do" list from God? Well, we know that God has things He wants each of us to do, but MY "To Do" list is going to look a lot different from *your* "To Do" list? Why? Because God gave each of us different things that we care about and are good at. The things that are unique about you, are the things that God wants you to use to get your "To Do" list done!

Callie has always cared about other people. When she sees someone who is sad, she HAS to try and help them feel better. She always seems to know the right thing to say to encourage someone. It just comes really easy for her!

It's no accident that Callie cares about people. God made her that way! When He created her, He put inside of her the gift of compassion – which helps her notice other people's feelings and care about helping them. God gave her that gift because He needed someone to make other people feel loved. So, God gave Callie the gift of compassion and wrote in SUPER HUGE letters on Callie's "To Do" list: CARE FOR PEOPLE!

Betsy couldn't be more different than Callie. She is pretty shy around other people, but she LOVES to spend time alone in her room reading books and writing. She could write in her journal for hours every day! She loves to play Scrabble, do crosswords and word finds, and spend time doing ANYTHING that has to do with words.

You know why God created Betsy with a love for words? Because He wanted her to write things. Books, letters, poems, stories… all kinds of things! God's "To Do" list for Betsy is to tell people about God by using words. And God's plan for her isn't just to use words when she's a grown up! Oh no! He wants her to start using her amazing gift right now! She writes beautiful poems that she shares with her friends. She writes incredible stories that she can share with her teacher and her class. God wants everyone to know how much He loves them, and Betsy is going to help Him get the word out.

And then there's Tana. Tana likes to be in charge. People seem to follow her and listen to the things she says. She likes making decisions and is always thinking of ways to make things better. And just like Betsy and Callie, it is NO accident that Tana is the way she is. You know why? Because God created her to be a LEADER. When He was creating her, He gave her the ability to inspire other people and help guide them. God needed someone who could direct other people to Him, and so he wrote LEAD on Tana's "To Do" list.

And that's just a few examples! There are hundreds of ways that God wants to use you. He has amazing things planned for you and He has given you everything you need to do His plan for your life!

But sometimes you and I can think we don't have a "To Do" list from God. We're not sure why we're here. We don't feel very important. We haven't figured out what's on our list, and so we just decide that God doesn't want to use us. Sometimes, we can even start thinking that God wants to use everyone EXCEPT us! But that is SOOOOO not true!

God has a plan for you! He will show you the things that He has planned for your life. You don't have to compare your list to anyone else's, because God made a list JUST for you.

And sometimes we don't think that we can really do what's on our list. We might feel scared or too small to do anything for God. You might wonder how in the world you could do something as important as telling other people about Jesus. But God promises to help you with every single thing He has planned for you.

There is a man in the Bible who wondered if he could really do everything that was on God's "To Do" list for his life. His name was Jeremiah. God came to him and said, *"Jeremiah, I am your Creator, and before you were born, I chose you to speak for me to the nations."* (Jeremiah 1:4-5 CEV)

Polka Dot Girls ❀ Who Am I?

week 5

Woah! Pretty big stuff. God showed Jeremiah what was on his list. In big ol' letters, Jeremiah's list said SPEAKER. God told him that even before he was born, that God knew Him and designed Him with the ability to speak to other people about God!

But Jeremiah wasn't so sure about this! He said, *"I'm not a good speaker, Lord, and I'm too young."* (Jeremiah 1:6 CEV) Just like many of us respond to God's list for us, Jeremiah had lots of reasons why he thought he wasn't good enough to do what God had asked him to do.

But God said something really amazing to Jeremiah. He said, *"Don't say you are too young. If I tell you to go and speak to someone, then go! And when I tell you what to say, don't leave out a word! I promise to be with you and keep you safe, so don't be afraid."* (Jeremiah 1:7-9 CEV)

God tells Jeremiah that he doesn't need to be afraid, because He will always be with him. He tells Jeremiah that he shouldn't worry about the words he will say, because God was going to put them right in his mouth! God makes it very clear to Jeremiah that He has a plan for His life, and that Jeremiah better get to it!

So, what do you think is on YOUR "To Do" list? What are the gifts that God has place in you? And how do you think He could use those things to help share His love with the world?

Think about the things you love. What do you get excited about? Helping your mom cook? Playing sports? Organizing things? Taking care of your little sister or brother? Reading? Doing crafts and making things? It's no accident that you love the things you love. God created you that way to help you with your "To Do" list!

What about the things you are good at? Maybe you LOVE math class. Or science or music? Are you really good at cleaning your room or helping your mom with the laundry? Maybe you are really good at the computer and you love to figure out all kinds of games and programs. It's no accident that you're good at the things you're good at. God created you that way to help you with your "To Do" list!

And what about the things that really bother you? Maybe you get really upset when you see someone getting picked on. Maybe you hear stories about children that live in other countries that don't have enough food and you just can't stop thinking about it. Do you find yourself concerned about the environment and taking care of the earth God gave us? Maybe you are really excited about buying Christmas gifts for kids who can't afford them every year. It's no accident that the things that bother you bother you! God created you that way to help you with your "To Do" list!

God is asking you to help Him. Before you were even born, He had a plan for your life. He wants you to help Him care for the people of the world. He is asking you to use the gifts He has given you to share His love. He wants the whole world to know about Him – and He's going to use YOU to do it. Pretty cool.

Closing Prayer: Dear God, Thank you for having a plan for my life. I want to tell others about you by using all the gifts you have given me. Help me to know what to do and what to say. I give you my life to do anything you ask of me. Thanks for letting me be a part of what you're doing. I love you. Amen.

week 5

Kindergarten and 1st Grade Group Discussion Questions

1. Has your Mom or Dad ever given you a "To Do" list? What are some of the things that they ask you to help with?

2. God has a "To Do" list for your life! What do you think that means?
    a. God has a plan for your life.
    b. There are things that God wants me to do for Him.
    c. I get to be God's helper!

3. What are some of the things that God wants us to do to help Him?
    a. Take care of people.
    b. Show God's love to people.
    c. Tell the world about Jesus.

4. When God created you, He put some things inside of you that would help you do your "To Do" list. What are some of the things that God put inside of you?

5. What are some of the things you love? What are some things you get excited about? (Let each girl give an idea or two.)

6. What are you good at?

7. What bothers you?

8. God has a plan for your life! Practice saying the theme verse together.

I know the plans I have in mind for you, declares the LORD; they are plans for peace, not disaster, to give you a future filled with hope.
– Jeremiah 29:11 (CEB)

Polka Dot Girls ❖ Who Am I?

week 5

2nd and 3rd Grade Group Discussion Questions

1. Has your Mom or Dad ever given you a "To Do" list? What are some of the things that they ask you to help with?

2. God has a "To Do" list for your life! What do you think that means?

    a. God has a plan for your life.

    b. There are things that God wants me to do for Him.

    c. I get to be God's helper!

3. What are some of the things that God wants us to do to help Him?

    a. Take care of people.

    b. Show God's love to people.

    c. Tell the world about Jesus.

4. When God created you, He put some things inside of you that would help you do your "To Do" list. What are some of the things that God put inside of you?

5. What are some of the things you love? What are some things you get excited about? (Let each girl give an idea or two.)

6. What are you good at?

7. What bothers you?

8. God has a plan for your life! Practice saying the theme verse together.

I know the plans I have in mind for you, declares the LORD; they are plans for peace, not disaster, to give you a future filled with hope.
– Jeremiah 29:11 (CEB)

Polka Dot Girls ❖ Who Am I?

week 5

4th and 5th Grade Group Discussion Questions

1. Has your Mom or Dad ever given you a "To Do" list? What are some of the things that they ask you to help with?

2. God has a "To Do" list for your life! What do you think that means?
   a. God has a plan for your life.
   b. There are things that God wants me to do for Him.
   c. I get to be God's helper!

3. What are some of the things that God wants us to do to help Him?
   a. Take care of people.
   b. Show God's love to people.
   c. Tell the world about Jesus.

4. Why do you think its easy to think God hasn't give you a list – or that you aren't good enough to do what's on it?
   a. We compare ourselves to other people.
   b. We aren't sure what we're good at.
   c. We don't think the things we're good at are important enough for God to use. (Like... How in the world could God use my ability to keep my room clean for anything important! But God uses everything about us to accomplish His plan for our lives – even if it seems insignificant to us!)

5. When God created you, He put some things inside of you that would help you do your "To Do" list. What are some of the things that God put inside of you?

6. What are some of the things you love? What are some things you get excited about? (Let each girl give an idea or two.)

7. What are you good at?

8. What bothers you?

8. God has a plan for your life! Practice saying the theme verse together.

I know the plans I have in mind for you, declares the LORD; they are plans for peace, not disaster, to give you a future filled with hope.
– Jeremiah 29:11 (CEB)

week 5

My "To Do" List Bookmark

<u>Supplies Needed:</u>

- Cardstock
- Hole punch
- Ribbon
- Markers/crayons
- Pretty embellishments (optional)

<u>Prep:</u>

- Copy the template on to your favorite color cardstock
- Cut out the bookmark

<u>What should we do?</u>

- Decorate the bookmark with markers/crayons and pretty embellishments.
- Punch a hole at the top of the bookmark.
- Thread ribbon through the hole and tie at the top.
- Write down your "To Do" list from God and keep it in your Bible or favorite book as a reminder to follow God's plan for your life!

My "To Do" List

My "To Do" List

My "To Do" List

My "To Do" List

Polka Dot Plus

week 5

Weekly Challenge

Grow: GROW your faith by reading Jeremiah 1:4-9

Love: What are some of the things you discovered about your "To Do" list today? How can you share the LOVE of God with someone by using the gift's God has given you?

Act: Pick one thing from your list and do it! Tell someone about Jesus. Show love to someone. Stand up for a person' who's being picked on. Write a poem talking about how much you love God. Whatever your gifts are… use them!

Memorize: MEMORIZE Jeremiah 29:11

I know the plans I have in mind for you, declares the LORD; they are plans for peace, not disaster, to give you a future filled with hope.

Parent Partner

We all can wonder what in the world we are supposed to do with our lives. I know it's a question I ask myself often! And your daughter is no different. Even if she may not be able to articulate it to you, we all need a sense of purpose and knowing where we fit into the larger picture.

God designed your daughter with an amazing set of traits and gifts that were uniquely designed to equip her to fulfill the purpose God has for her life. It's no accident that she loves to paint or sing or run or organize things! In the grand design of our grand Creator, she was formed and fashioned for her purpose.

It's never too early to start drawing out the gifts in your children. And it's not just talents I'm talking about here – your daughter has been given spiritual gifts by God! 1Peter 4:10 says, *"God has given each one of you a gift from his great variety of spiritual gifts. Use them well to serve one another."* She's got them! Perhaps it is the gift of compassion or leadership or teaching. Maybe she has the gift of serving or giving. Ask God to show you how He uniquely designed your daughter.

And then begin to develop those gifts in her! If she has the gift of service, find ways for her to serve in your home and even in your community. If she has a compassionate heart, provide opportunities for her to care for other people. (Compassion kids do really great with pets… So if you're up for it……..) Look for opportunities to call out the gifts you see in her and encourage her that God has great big plans for her life.

week 5

Kindergarten and 1st Grade Take Home Activity Sheet

God gave us the things we're good at as a gift in order to do our "To Do" list? Circle your top three favorite things to do to figure out your Spiritual Gifts!

1. I love to plan and organize.

ADMINISTRATION

2. I love to draw and do crafts.

CREATIVE

3. I love to encourage people who are having a hard time.

ENCOURAGEMENT

4. I love to tell people about Jesus.

EVANGELISM

5. I love to share.

GIVING

6. I love to make people feel welcome.

HOSPITALITY

7. I love to pray for people.

PRAYER

8. I love to take the lead in the classroom.

LEADERSHIP

9. I love to take care of people who are in need.

MERCY

10. I love to do things for other people.

HELPS

11. I love to teach.

TEACHING

Polka Dot Girls ❀ Who Am I?

week 5

2nd and 3rd Grade Take Home Activity Sheet

Spiritual Gifts Survey

Directions: Please rate yourself from 3 to 0. For each sentence, circle **ONE** number that represents you best.

Rating Scale:
  3 is something you always do
  2 is something you do most of the time
  1 is something you do once in a while
  0 is something you have never done

1. I like to organize	3 2 1 0
2. I like to create things and make crafts	3 2 1 0
3. I like to see the best in people	3 2 1 0
4. I like to share Jesus with others	3 2 1 0
5. I find it easy to trust God to answer my prayers	3 2 1 0
6. I like to give my money to people in need	3 2 1 0
7. I enjoy doing basic tasks for other people	3 2 1 0
8. I like to make people feel welcome	3 2 1 0
9. I like to make plans	3 2 1 0
10. I like to care for others	3 2 1 0
11. I like to pray for other people	3 2 1 0

12. I like to teach God's Word to others	3 2 1 0
13. I am careful and can manage a lot of details	3 2 1 0
14. I like to use my artistic skills in art, drama, music, dance, etc.	3 2 1 0
15. I like helping people feel better when they are sad or discouraged	3 2 1 0
16. I am concerned for people who don't believe in God	3 2 1 0
17. I believe God is always with me even when I am having a hard time	3 2 1 0
18. I like to tithe to my church	3 2 1 0
19. I like to help at my church	3 2 1 0
20. I like to help new kids connect at school or church	3 2 1 0
21. I can motivate people to reach a goal	3 2 1 0
22. I am patient with people who are having a hard time	3 2 1 0
23. I enjoy praying for long periods of time	3 2 1 0
24. I like to study and share what I have learned with others	3 2 1 0
25. I like to make "To Do" lists and complete it	3 2 1 0
26. I like to share God with others through art, music or dance	3 2 1 0
27. I like to help people feel courageous when they are afraid	3 2 1 0
28. I am not afraid to share Jesus with others	3 2 1 0
29. I trust God with everything I do	3 2 1 0
30. I like to share what I have with my friends and family	3 2 1 0
31. I like to find things that need to be done and do them without being asked	3 2 1 0

week 5

32. I enjoy having friends over to my house   3 2 1 0

33. I like to set up a plan to achieve my goals   3 2 1 0

34. I like to help people who others have ignored or rejected   3 2 1 0

35. When I hear about something sad or a person in need,
    I pray right away   3 2 1 0

36. I like to tell stories   3 2 1 0

37. I like to help others get organized   3 2 1 0

38. I like to use my imagination   3 2 1 0

39. I like to encourage others who may be unsure if
    they believe in God   3 2 1 0

40. I like to find opportunities to share my faith with
    people who don't believe in God   3 2 1 0

41. I believe God will help me do great things   3 2 1 0

42. I like to give my money to those in need rather than
    put it in spend it on myself   3 2 1 0

43. I like to help my family, friends or teachers to get things done   3 2 1 0

44. I like to do whatever I can to make people feel like they belong   3 2 1 0

45. I figure out what needs to be done and I do it   3 2 1 0

46. I have great compassion for hurting people   3 2 1 0

47. I feel honored when someone asks me to pray for them   3 2 1 0

48. I find it easy to explain things to others   3 2 1 0

Results:

- Write your score for each number (1-48) in the tables below.
- Add the numbers for each gift and put it in the total colum.
- Circle the top three scores. These are your strongest gifts.

ADMINISTRATION	CREATIVE ARTS	ENCOURAGEMENT	EVANGELISM
1 _____	2 _____	3 _____	4 _____
13 _____	14 _____	15 _____	16 _____
25 _____	26 _____	27 _____	28 _____
37 _____	38 _____	39 _____	40 _____
Total _____	Total _____	Total _____	Total _____

FAITH	GIVING	HELPS	HOSPITALITY
5 _____	6 _____	7 _____	8 _____
17 _____	18 _____	19 _____	20 _____
29 _____	30 _____	31 _____	32 _____
41 _____	42 _____	43 _____	44 _____
Total _____	Total _____	Total _____	Total _____

LEADERSHIP	MERCY	PRAYER	TEACHING
9 _____	10 _____	11 _____	12 _____
21 _____	22 _____	23 _____	24 _____
33 _____	34 _____	35 _____	36 _____
45 _____	46 _____	47 _____	48 _____
Total _____	Total _____	Total _____	Total _____

My 3 Strongest Spiritual Gifts

Gift 1 _____ Gift 2 _____ Gift 3 _____

week 5

4th and 5th Grade Take Home Activity Sheet

SPIRITUAL GIFTS SURVEY

Directions: Please rate yourself from 3 to 0. For each sentence, circle **ONE** number that represents you best.

Rating Scale:

   3 is something you always do

   2 is something you do most of the time

   1 is something you do once in a while

   0 is something you have never done

1. I like to organize	3 2 1 0
2. I like to create things and make crafts	3 2 1 0
3. I like to see the best in people	3 2 1 0
4. I like to share Jesus with others	3 2 1 0
5. I find it easy to trust God to answer my prayers	3 2 1 0
6. I like to give my money to people in need	3 2 1 0
7. I enjoy doing basic tasks for other people	3 2 1 0
8. I like to make people feel welcome	3 2 1 0
9. I like to make plans	3 2 1 0
10. I like to care for others	3 2 1 0
11. I like to pray for other people	3 2 1 0

12. I like to teach God's Word to others   3 2 1 0

13. I am careful and can manage a lot of details   3 2 1 0

14. I like to use my artistic skills in art, drama, music, dance, etc.   3 2 1 0

15. I like helping people feel better when they are sad or discouraged   3 2 1 0

16. I am concerned for people who don't believe in God   3 2 1 0

17. I believe God is always with me even when I am having
    a hard time   3 2 1 0

18. I like to tithe to my church   3 2 1 0

19. I like to help at my church   3 2 1 0

20. I like to help new kids connect at school or church   3 2 1 0

21. I can motivate people to reach a goal   3 2 1 0

22. I am patient with people who are having a hard time   3 2 1 0

23. I enjoy praying for long periods of time   3 2 1 0

24. I like to study and share what I have learned with others   3 2 1 0

25. I like to make "To Do" lists and complete it   3 2 1 0

26. I like to share God with others through art, music or dance   3 2 1 0

27. I like to help people feel courageous when they are afraid   3 2 1 0

28. I am not afraid to share Jesus with others   3 2 1 0

29. I trust God with everything I do   3 2 1 0

30. I like to share what I have with my friends and family   3 2 1 0

31. I like to find things that need to be done and do
    them without being asked   3 2 1 0

week 5

32. I enjoy having friends over to my house　　　　　　　　　　　3 2 1 0

33. I like to set up a plan to achieve my goals　　　　　　　　　　3 2 1 0

34. I like to help people who others have ignored or rejected　　　3 2 1 0

35. When I hear about something sad or a person in need,
　　I pray right away　　　　　　　　　　　　　　　　　　　　3 2 1 0

36. I like to tell stories　　　　　　　　　　　　　　　　　　　　3 2 1 0

37. I like to help others get organized　　　　　　　　　　　　　3 2 1 0

38. I like to use my imagination　　　　　　　　　　　　　　　　3 2 1 0

39. I like to encourage others who may be unsure if
　　they believe in God　　　　　　　　　　　　　　　　　　　3 2 1 0

40. I like to find opportunities to share my faith with
　　people who don't believe in God　　　　　　　　　　　　　3 2 1 0

41. I believe God will help me do great things　　　　　　　　　3 2 1 0

42. I like to give my money to those in need rather than
　　put it in spend it on myself　　　　　　　　　　　　　　　3 2 1 0

43. I like to help my family, friends or teachers to get things done　3 2 1 0

44. I like to do whatever I can to make people feel like they belong　3 2 1 0

45. I figure out what needs to be done and I do it　　　　　　　3 2 1 0

46. I have great compassion for hurting people　　　　　　　　　3 2 1 0

47. I feel honored when someone asks me to pray for them　　　3 2 1 0

48. I find it easy to explain things to others　　　　　　　　　　3 2 1 0

Results:

- Write your score for each number (1-48) in the tables below.
- Add the numbers for each gift and put it in the total column.
- Circle the top three scores. These are your strongest gifts.

ADMINISTRATION	CREATIVE ARTS	ENCOURAGEMENT	EVANGELISM
1 _____	2 _____	3 _____	4 _____
13 _____	14 _____	15 _____	16 _____
25 _____	26 _____	27 _____	28 _____
37 _____	38 _____	39 _____	40 _____
Total _____	Total _____	Total _____	Total _____

FAITH	GIVING	HELPS	HOSPITALITY
5 _____	6 _____	7 _____	8 _____
17 _____	18 _____	19 _____	20 _____
29 _____	30 _____	31 _____	32 _____
41 _____	42 _____	43 _____	44 _____
Total _____	Total _____	Total _____	Total _____

LEADERSHIP	MERCY	PRAYER	TEACHING
9 _____	10 _____	11 _____	12 _____
21 _____	22 _____	23 _____	24 _____
33 _____	34 _____	35 _____	36 _____
45 _____	46 _____	47 _____	48 _____
Total _____	Total _____	Total _____	Total _____

My 3 Strongest Spiritual Gifts

Gift 1 _____ Gift 2 _____ Gift 3 _____

Who Am I?

week 6

God Confidence

WHAT'S THE POINT?

OUR CONFIDENCE ISN'T IN WHAT WE CAN DO, WHAT OTHER PEOPLE THINK OF US, OR EVEN WHAT WE THINK OF OURSELVES. OUR CONFIDENCE IS IN GOD.

theme verse

For you have been my hope, Sovereign LORD, my confidence since my youth.
Psalm 71:5 NIV

related bible story

Philippians 3

❋ Large Group Lesson ❋

Sally had a problem. Her teacher had asked her to lead an after school book club. She announced to the whole class that Sally would be in charge of the group – choosing the books, organizing the meetings and leading the discussion time. Now, Sally LOVED to read, but the teacher was asking her to do something WAY different than just read a book! She was asking her to be in charge of something!

All she could think of was, "What if no one comes?" "What if no one likes my ideas?" "What if I don't know what to say?" "What if my hair looks silly that day and everyone is staring at me?" "What if I actually pass out from nervousness right in front of everyone?!" Sally was not feeling very confident about herself at the moment.

WHAT IS CONFIDENCE?

Confidence is believing that you can do something. It's knowing that you can do anything. It's feeling strong and sure about yourself and your abilities. It's being okay with who you are, what you can do and holding your head up high.

The last thing Sally was feeling was confident! All she could think of were the reasons why she couldn't do it. And the more she thought about it, the more she doubted herself and just wanted to quit the whole thing altogether.

Have you ever felt really confident about something? Maybe you are really good at a certain thing, and when you do it, you feel proud and strong inside. Maybe you feel confident when you step out onto a soccer field. Maybe you feel confident when you are playing the piano. Maybe you feel confident when you're doing homework or taking a test.

And what about times when you HAVEN'T felt confident?! I'm sure you can think of a few of those! When you have to try something new? When you have to do something that you're NOT very good at? When you are around new people and you're not sure what they're going to think of you? There are LOTS of moments when I don't feel very confident.

So, what's the key to being confident? What would you say if I told you that there was a way for you to feel confident no matter what you were doing, where you were doing it, or who was around? Can you imagine? I want some of that confidence!!!

There IS a way for you to have confidence in every single situation you face. There IS a way for you to feel strong in every job or task you find in your hands. And there IS a way to feel confident about who you are, what you look like and your place on the earth.

How?

By finding your confidence in God.

Polka Dot Girls ❀ Who Am I?

I know that might sound confusing. How can I find confidence in myself by finding confidence in God? Well, when we give our lives to God, and we belong to Him, everything we say and do is wrapped up in Him. Sally was asked to lead book club because God planned it for her! And because God planned it for her, He is going to help her do her very best. He's going to help her pick the right book. He's going to give her the words to say for the discussion time. He's going to give her ideas and direction. Knowing that God will never let her down, and has promised to help her no matter what she's doing should give Sally GREAT confidence! He NEVER messes up – and if He's going to help her – then she's going to do a great job!

The truth is, most of us try and feel confident in the wrong thing. We look to lots of different things to make us feel secure and strong, but most of those things end up leaving us LESS confident!

Let's talk about a few of them.

First of all, many of us try to have:

➡ 1. SELF-CONFIDENCE.

Have you ever heard that word before? A lot of people talk about having self-confidence. Self-confidence is believing in yourself. Now, I bet you're wondering why in the world that would be a bad thing! Well, it's not a bad thing. It's awesome to feel good about yourself and the things you are good at doing. God doesn't want you feeling bad about yourself. He is your biggest cheerleader – He wants you to be strong, confident and secure.

But I'll tell you why self-confidence can be a tricky thing. Why does Sally feel good about herself when she's READING a book, but not when she has to lead a discussion about a book? Sally knows that she's good at reading. She is self-confident in her ability to read quickly and understand what she is reading. But she DOESN'T feel self-confident about her ability to lead a group.

It's a GOOD thing for Sally to be proud of her reading skills, but if that's the only way she's going to feel confident about herself, she's going to be pretty limited in what she feels good about! What about all the times she has to do

things that she's not super good at? What about the times when she has to try a new thing? Unfortunately, being confident in yourself leaves you feeling good about only a few things that you are good at and the rest of the time you are going to feel awful.

There was a man in the Bible named Paul who learned to not be confident in the things he was good at. And man, oh man, was he good at a lot of things. He was a very successful man who had studied at the best schools, came from the best family, hung around with the most important people and held a high position. There was a time when Paul didn't know God, and he was very proud and confident in all his abilities and strengths.

But then something amazing happened. Paul found Jesus. He had an incredible, life-changing encounter with God and became one of the greatest missionaries ever who shared Jesus with countless people and even wrote a large part of the Bible we read today!

Paul wrote these words in Philippians 3:3, "*We put no confidence in human effort, though I could have confidence in my own effort if anyone could.*" Paul learned that even though he was good at a lot of things, that he couldn't put his confidence in himself. He had to keep his eyes on God.

I don't know about you, but I want to feel confident in ALL the areas of my life, not just the things I'm good at. When I keep my eyes on myself and what I am able to do, I usually feel overwhelmed and discouraged.

But when I stop and look to God and His promise to help me with everything I ever need, I can walk into any situation with the confidence that God is going to help me. I remember what the Bible says in Philippians 4:13, "*I can do everything through Christ who strengthens me.*"

Also, God wants us to rely on Him! When we begin to rely on ourselves, we miss a huge part of who God wants to be in our lives! He wants to be our helper. He wants us to always look to Him for strength and courage. When we feel like we can do it ourselves, we start to think we don't need God.

Polka Dot Girls ❀ Who Am I?

week 6

It's like my little girl, Dottie who is three years old. She always says to me, "I do it myself!" Now, she THINKS she can do everything herself, but the truth is, she needs my help! I can teach her how to do new things and show her the right way. When she won't let me help her, she's missing out on a lot! And when we start to be confident in our own abilities, instead of relying on God, we are saying, "I do it myself!" We could do so much more, and He could show us so many new and awesome things if we'd just let Him help us, but for many of us, our self-reliance makes us think we don't need His help.

We need to replace our self-confidence with a reliance on God.

Self-confidence says, "I can do that!" But God confidence says, "God will help me do that."

Another way that we find confidence in the wrong place, is by trying to have

⇨ 2. People Confidence

Karen's parents were very encouraging. They were constantly telling her how beautiful and talented she was. They were always pointing out what a good job she had done on things, and how proud of her they were. She always felt confident around her family.

And then along came Mrs. Burkus. Mrs. Burkus was Karen's second grade teacher and Mrs. Burkus was NOT encouraging. At all. She never told Karen she was doing a good job. She always pointed out the ways Karen could have done better. She didn't compliment her on her new outfit or tell her she appreciated her help with the lunch count every day.

Karen felt HORRIBLE every time she had to walk into Mrs. Burkus' classroom. She hated being there. No matter how well she did on her work, she always felt like she wasn't doing a good job because Mrs. Burkus didn't encourage her.

Pretty soon, Karen didn't just feel bad about herself in Mrs. Burkus' classroom, she was feeling bad about herself all the time. Why didn't her teacher like her? Why didn't she say nice things to her? She just couldn't help thinking that if Mrs. Burkus didn't like her, then she must not be very likeable.

Has that ever happened to you? Maybe you don't have "Mrs. Burkus," but maybe you have someone else who hasn't been very nice to you and suddenly you find your confidence GONE! It's sure happened to me. I have found myself feeling nervous and self-conscious about areas I used to feel really confident in because of something someone else said to me.

And you know why that happened to me? Because I was trying to find self-confidence in other people. I felt good about myself when THEY felt good about me. I felt good about my abilities when THEY felt good about my abilities. If they were happy with me, then I was happy with myself. Blech.

That is no fun – and it is not the way God wants you to live your life. That is why He tells us to only put our confidence in Him and not other people. Psalm 146:3 says, "*Don't put your confidence in powerful people.*" We are not suppose to look to other people to make us feel strong, secure, or confident. That's God's job… and we're not supposed to try and get anyone else to do God's job for Him!

When you are looking to other people to make you feel confident, you constantly have to be thinking about what would make THEM happy or what THEY would want you to say or do instead of wondering what would make GOD happy or what GOD wants you to do. The Bible tells us that we aren't supposed to put pleasing other people above pleasing God. Galatians 1:10 says, "*Obviously, I'm not trying to win the approval of people, but of God. If pleasing people were my goal, I would not be Christ's servant.*" I want to please God, don't you? And we cannot please God if we're too worried about pleasing other people.

When you are feeling nervous or insecure about something, ask yourself this question: "What does God think of me?" "Is what I'm doing making Him happy?" "Is this something He wants me to do?" Then remind yourself that if He has asked you to do something, it's because He believes in you and is going to help you do the very best job you can. If He is happy with you, then you can have all the confidence in the world in spite of what other people may think or say about you. Remember what is says in Psalm 18:8: "*It is better to trust and take refuge in the Lord than to put confidence in man.*" (AMP)

Polka Dot Girls ❀ Who Am I?

Sally had to realize that she couldn't change Mrs. Burkus. She had to realize that just because Mrs. Burkus wasn't encouraging her, didn't mean she didn't like her or believe in her. And EVEN IF IT DID, Mrs. Burkus' opinion of her didn't matter because she knew that God had made her smart and talented and that HE believed in her. That was all she needed.

It can be so easy to put our confidence in ourselves or look to find it in other people's opinions of us. But God wants you to simply find your confidence in HIM. Trust that He believes in you. Trust that He is always with you. Trust that He will give you the strength to do ANYTHING He asks of you.

I want to leave you today with a letter written by our good old buddy Paul. He wrote these words in 2 Thessalonians 2:15. *"So, friends, take a firm stand, feet on the ground and head high. Keep a tight grip on what you were taught, whether in personal conversation or by our letter. May Jesus himself and God our Father, who reached out in love and surprised you with gifts of unending help and confidence, put a fresh heart in you, invigorate your work, enliven your speech."* (MSG)

God believes in you. That's all the confidence you need.

Polka Dot Girls ❀ Who Am I?

week 6

Kindergarten and 1st Grade Group Discussion Questions

1. What does "confidence" mean?

   a. Confidence is believing that you can do something.

   b. It's knowing that you can do anything.

   c. It's feeling strong and sure about yourself and your abilities.

   d. It's being okay with who you are, what you can do and holding your head up high.

2. Is there something you feel really confident about doing? Or something about yourself that you feel confident about? Share with the group.

3. What about something you **DON'T** feel confident about? Maybe something that makes you really nervous or anxious or something in which you're not very sure of yourself?

4. What does it mean to have "God Confidence?"

   a. We can be confident in who God made us to be.

   b. We can trust that HE will help us with anything He asks us to do.

   c. We can know that He will never fail us or let us down.

   d. We can be sure of ourselves no matter what anyone else says or thinks because we know that God thinks we are amazing!

5. What is wrong with "self-confidence?"

   a. If we're only confident in the things we're good at, we're going to be left with a lot of areas of our life we're NOT confident in.

   b. We can't rely on our own strength and abilities, we need to trust God to help us.

   c. When we start to trust in ourselves, we aren't relying on God… and He **ALWAYS** wants us relying on Him.

6. Why should we not try and gain confidence through other people?

   a. We shouldn't base our opinion of ourselves on what other people think of us.

   b. We need to please God, and when we're looking to other people for our confidence, we will try to please them instead.

7. Practice saying this week's theme verse together:

   "For you have been my hope, Sovereign LORD, my confidence since my youth."
   Psalm 71:5 NIV

week 6

2nd and 3rd Grade Group Discussion Questions

1. What does "confidence" mean?

    a. Confidence is believing that you can do something.

    b. It's knowing that you can do anything.

    c. It's feeling strong and sure about yourself and your abilities.

    d. It's being okay with who you are, what you can do and holding your head up high.

2. Is there something you feel really confident about doing? Or something about yourself that you feel confident about? Share with the group.

3. What about something you DON'T feel confident about? Maybe something that makes you really nervous or anxious or something in which you're not very sure of yourself?

4. What does it mean to have "God Confidence?"

    a. We can be confident in who God made us to be.

    b. We can trust that HE will help us with anything He asks us to do.

    c. We can know that He will never fail us or let us down.

    d. We can be sure of ourselves no matter what anyone else says or thinks because we know that God thinks we are amazing!

5. What is wrong with "self-confidence?"

    a. If we're only confident in the things we're good at, we're going to be left with a lot of areas of our life we're NOT confident in.

    b. We can't rely on our own strength and abilities, we need to trust God to help us.

    c. When we start to trust in ourselves, we aren't relying on God... and He ALWAYS wants us relying on Him.

6. Why should we not try and gain confidence through other people?

    a. We shouldn't base our opinion of ourselves on what other people think of us.

    b. We need to please God, and when we're looking to other people for our confidence, we will try to please them instead.

7. Practice saying this week's theme verse together:

    "For you have been my hope, Sovereign LORD, my confidence since my youth."
    Psalm 71:5 NIV

week 6

4th and 5th Grade Group Discussion Questions

1. What does "confidence" mean?

   a. Confidence is believing that you can do something.

   b. It's knowing that you can do anything.

   c. It's feeling strong and sure about yourself and your abilities.

   d. It's being okay with who you are, what you can do and holding your head up high.

2. Is there something you feel really confident about doing? Or something about yourself that you feel confident about? Share with the group.

3. What about something you **DON'T** feel confident about? Maybe something that makes you really nervous or anxious or something in which you're not very sure of yourself?

4. What does it mean to have "God Confidence?"

   a. We can be confident in who God made us to be.

   b. We can trust that HE will help us with anything He asks us to do.

   c. We can know that He will never fail us or let us down.

   d. We can be sure of ourselves no matter what anyone else says or thinks because we know that God thinks we are amazing!

5. What is wrong with "self-confidence?"

   a. If we're only confident in the things we're good at, we're going to be left with a lot of areas of our life we're NOT confident in.

   b. We can't rely on our own strength and abilities, we need to trust God to help us.

   c. When we start to trust in ourselves, we aren't relying on God... and He **ALWAYS** wants us relying on Him.

6. Why should we not try and gain confidence through other people?

   a. We shouldn't base our opinion of ourselves on what other people think of us.

   b. We need to please God, and when we're looking to other people for our confidence, we will try to please them instead.

7. Practice saying this week's theme verse together:

   "For you have been my hope, Sovereign LORD, my confidence since my youth."
   Psalm 71:5 NIV

week 6

God Confidence Foam Bracelets!

Leaders: Make sure you do adequate preparation for the crafts in accordance to the age and skill level of your group. For younger children, attach the velcro to the bracelets. Older children should be able to add the velcro and decorate the bracelet in the allotted time.

Supplies Needed:

- Scraps of foam
- Small foam shapes (hearts, flowers, etc.)
- Self-adhesive jewels
- Self-adhesive velcro tabs
- Black permanent markers

Prep:

- Cut foam into strips of 1 to 1 ½" wide and long enough to fit around your girls' wrist.
- Leave a 1" overlap for fastening.

What should we do?

- Stick the velcro fastener onto the short end of the foam strip so that it overlaps to form a clasp.
- Decorate the bracelet with foam shapes and jewels.
- Write on the bracelet **"Phil 4:13"** to remember that you can do anything with God's strength!

Polka Dot Girls ❖ Who Am I?

Polka Dot Plus

week 6

Weekly Challenge

Grow: Read the story of Paul's conversion in Acts 9.

Love: If you see someone who is not very confident (maybe a friend or a sibling) encourage them. Tell them that you KNOW that God believes in them and will help them!

Act: Think of an area where you haven't confident. Ask God to help you, and then take one step forward in that area.

Maybe that means saying "yes" to a new adventure. Maybe it means trying out for something you have been afraid to try. Believe that God will help you – and then GO FOR IT!

Memorize: Memorize this week's theme verse: *For you have been my hope, Sovereign LORD, my confidence since my youth.* – Psalm 71:5 NIV

Parent Partner

Okay. So I realize that your daughter may or may not come to you tonight and tell you that she learned from Polka Dot Girls that's she shouldn't be self-confident. And I realize that right now you may or may not wonder if I have lost my mind. Let me answer you…. quickly… before you chuck this book out the window.

Our children are taught in many, many places that they need to have confidence in themselves. And this is true! I deeply want our daughters (and sons for that matter) to feel good about their abilities and who they are. But there is a dangerous balance to be achieved in the area of "self-confidence." We want to encourage children to believe in themselves, and yet we also need to instill in them an absolute need to rely on God for everything. We want them to feel good about their unique talents, but if they only feel confident in the things they are good at, where does that leave them in the things they AREN'T good at? And we want them to believe in themselves, but far above that, we want them to believe in a God who has promise to help them achieve EXCEEDINGLY, ABUNDANTLY, MORE than they could ever hope to do in their own strength.

And so, instilling a GOD confidence in them instead of a SELF-confidence, is giving them a place to go to when they AREN'T good at something and when they DON'T feel sure of themselves. Encouraging them to look to God for their worth and value and strength instead of looking to other people for validation and security will instill in them a sense that it is far greater to please God than to please other people.

If you give your daughter the gift of GOD-CONFIDENCE, you are giving her a place to run to with every insecurity, inadequacy and temptation. She needs to learn to rely on HIS role in her life – and find her confidence in her relationship with Him.

SELF-confidence is fleeting.
PEOPLE-confidence is dangerous.
GOD-confidence is unfailing.

Polka Dot Girls ❧ Who Am I?

week 6

Kindergarten and 1st Grade
Take Home Activity Sheet

God confidence says, "God will help me do that!" In the space provided, draw a picture of yourself doing something you are afraid to do. With God-confidence you can do it!

You can always put your confidence in God and trust Him completely.

Read each verse below and write the word TRUST in the blank spaces. All scripture NIV.

Lord, those who know you will _____ in you. You have never deserted those who look to you. – Psalm 9:10

When I'm afraid, I will _____ in you. – Psalm 56:3

You are the King and the Lord. You have always been my hope. I have _____ed in you ever since I was young. – Psalm 71:5

But blessed is the one who _____ in the LORD, whose confidence is in him. – Jeremiah 17:6-8

"_____ in the Lord forever. The Lord is the Rock. The Lord will keep us safe forever. – Isaiah 26:4

Polka Dot Girls ❀ Who Am I?

week 6

2nd and 3rd Grade Take Home Activity Sheet

You can always put your confidence in God and trust Him completely. To find out what **Jeremiah 17:7** NIV says about having God-confidence, do the math problem to get a numerical answer. Then look at the code below to find the letter for each blank.

1 = A	2 = B	3 = C	4 = D	5 = E	6 = F	7 = G	8 = H
9 = I	10 = J	11 = K	12 = L	13 = M	14 = N	15 = O	16 = P
17 = Q	18 = R	19 = S	20 = T	21 = U	22 = V	23 = W	24 = X
25 = Y	26 = Z						

___ ___ ___   ___ ___ ___ ___ ___ ___ ___   ___ ___
1+1 16+5 25-5 5-3 6+6 10-5 20-1 14+5 6-1 1+3   12-3 17+2

___ ___ ___   ___ ___ ___   ___ ___ ___
26-6 6+2 15-10 13+2 28-14 8-3 20+3 4+4 7+8

___ ___ ___ ___ ___ ___   ___ ___   ___ ___ ___
22-2 9+9 16+5 10+9 8+12 20-1 6+3 12+2 16+4 15-7 1+4

___ ___ ___ ___ , ___ ___ ___ ___ ___
17-5 2+13 20-2 13-9   13+10 10-2 1+14 10+9 25-20

___ ___ ___ ___ ___ ___ ___ ___ ___ ___ ___ ___ ___ ___
1+2 20-5 9+5 3+3 4+5 6-2 16-11 7+7 6-3 7-2 18-9 12+7 11-2 8+6

___ ___ ___ . – Jeremiah 17:7 NIV
4+4 19-10 6+7

Word List

LORD	is	the	him	is
blessed	trusts	confidence	in	in
whose	who	one	the	

Polka Dot Girls ❀ Who Am I?

week 6

4th and 5th Grade Take Home Activity Sheet

The key to confidence is to _____ _____ _____.

To find the answer to the question:
- Look up each of the verses below in your Bible. All scripture NIV.
- Fill in the blank
- Circle the first letter of the word you put in the blank to discover the key to confidence.

When I am afraid, I put my _____ in you. – Psalm 56:3

Let us then approach God's throne of grace with confidence, so that we may _____ mercy and find grace to help us in our time of need. – Hebrews 4:16

Like a broken tooth or a lame foot is reliance on the _____ in a time of trouble. – Proverbs 25:19

For you have been my hope, _____ LORD, my confidence since my youth. – Psalm 71:5

Such confidence we have _____ Christ before God. – 2 Corinthians 3:4

For it is we who are the circumcision, we who serve God by his Spirit, who boast in Christ Jesus, and who put no confidence _____ the flesh. – Philippians 3:3

Should _____ your piety be your confidence and your blameless ways your hope? – Job 4:6

My heart, O _____, is steadfast, my heart is steadfast; I will sing and make music. – Psalm 57:7

But blessed is the _____ who trusts in the LORD, whose confidence is in him. – Jeremiah 17:7

I can _____ all this through him who gives me strength. – Philippians 4:13

Word List:

unfaithful	*God*	*not*	*receive*
trust	*in*	*through*	
Sovereign	*do*	*one*	

Who Am I?

week 7

So Much STUFF!

WHAT'S THE POINT?
GOD WANTS YOU TO LOVE HIM MORE THAN YOUR STUFF.

theme verse
"For where your treasure is, there your heart will be also."
Matthew 6:21 (NIV)

related bible story
Luke 18:18-23

❋ Large Group Lesson ❋

Kirsten was NOT looking forward to going back to school on Monday. It was the first day back after Christmas vacation, and she knew that everyone was going to be talking about all the amazing gifts they got. "Oh my goodness! You got the brand new whatchamacallit and so-and-so? So did I!! But I got one in every color so I could have OPTIONS!" New bikes, games, dolls, computers, toys… you name it, they got it. It's not like she wasn't happy for them, but every year the same thing would happen. Eventually, someone would ask her what SHE got for Christmas.

And this is the point where Kirsten wanted to crawl under her desk and hide. You see, Kirsten's dad had been out of work for a really long time. Actually, Kirsten couldn't remember a time when her dad HAD a job. He had been sick and it was just too difficult for him to work. Her mom had a job, but it didn't pay very

much money and most of the money she made went to pay her dad's medical bills.

So, Christmas at her house was just not the same as all her friends. Her parents would get her one small gift that usually didn't cost very much money. She was thankful for what she was given, but when she compared it to the piles of gifts everyone else from school got, she couldn't help but feel sad and embarrassed. Why couldn't her family have more money? And why couldn't she bear to tell anyone what was going on at home? She was so scared that people wouldn't like her because she didn't have much money.

Madison was in a completely different situation. Madison's family *did* have a lot of money. She always had lots of presents under the Christmas tree and if she wanted something, her parent's usually bought it for her. All her friends loved to come to her house because of all the cool things she had in her room and all the awesome toys and games she had.

But after a while, Madison started feeling like her friends only wanted to come over because of all her stuff. She didn't feel like they really cared about her. She wondered if people would still want to spend time with her if she didn't have all the fun things at her house. Why didn't people want to know her simply for who she was? Were people just trying to be her friend because of the things she had? She was so scared that people wouldn't like her if she didn't have money.

And then there's Marie. Marie's family wasn't really poor, but they weren't really rich either. She couldn't get everything she wanted, but her Mom and Dad were able to buy her lots of nice things. Most days, Marie didn't feeling very good about herself, but as soon as she put on a new cute shirt or a fancy pair of shoes, she suddenly felt more confident. When she had a new backpack or a fun new necklace, it made her feel like people would notice her. She didn't feel quite as nervous when she had something new to wear or show her friends.

The problem was that Marie was starting to rely on **STUFF** to make her feel confident. Instead of being happy with who God made her to be, she was using **THINGS** to try and make herself feel confident. What would she do if suddenly she had to face a new situation without a new outfit to help her feel more comfortable? What would she

do if she had to let people see her without all the new flashy things to get attention? She was so scared that she would have to face the world without all her STUFF.

Have you ever felt bad because you wanted something but couldn't have it? Have you ever felt embarrassed because you didn't have a certain kind of clothes or a certain toy or game that all your friends have? Or maybe you have a lot of nice things and you find yourself getting caught up in all the STUFF in your life. You feel like people don't see you – just the cool things you have. Or maybe you're relying on your stuff to make you feel confident or likeable.

It is really, really easy to get caught up in our STUFF. The stuff we HAVE and the stuff we DON'T HAVE. We can feel like we're not as good as other girls if we don't have the stuff they have. We can feel like people only like us for our stuff. And sometimes we can start to rely on our STUFF to make us feel good about ourselves instead of just being okay with who we are.

Believe it or not, the Bible talks a lot about STUFF. Well, you might not actually find the word STUFF in the Bible, but the idea of money and things comes up A LOT! You see, Jesus knew how big of a deal money and things could become in our lives.

WHO KNEW?

There are more verses in the Bible that talk about money than about love. There are well over 1,000 verses about money!

The problem with STUFF is that we can get SO wrapped up in the things we have and don't have, that it can become too important to us. Matthew 6:21 tells us *"For where your treasure is, there your heart will be also."* (NIV)

A treasure is something that is really important to you. It's the thing that you spend the most time and energy thinking about. Our treasure is what is closest to our hearts. God wants our hearts to be His! He wants us to trust Him and love Him and think about Him. But when we become too concerned with our STUFF, when our STUFF becomes our treasure, then our hearts belong to our STUFF instead of to God.

ILLUSTRATION: You will need:
- Large piece of cardboard or foam core
- Red paint
- Large black marker
- Pictures from magazine or catalog
- Hole punch
- Long pieces of string

You may need a helper or two to hold the heart while you work on it.

Prep:

Cut out a large foam or cardboard heart and paint it red. Then cut out some pictures of things that the girls might be interested in from catalogs or magazines *(American girl doll, new clothes, shoes, toys, CDs, anything trendy and fun)* Punch a hole in the picture and tie a LONG piece of string to it.

Illustration:
(Hold up the red heart.)

You know, girls, Deuteronomy 6:5 says that we are to *"Love the Lord your God with all your heart."* That means that we are to love GOD more than anything else. That our hearts belong to HIM alone. *(As you say this, write the word GOD in big letters on the heart.)*

But sometimes our STUFF can become too important to us.

(Hold up each picture separately. As you hold up each picture, show it to the girls, describe it in a fun and exciting manner, and you should get some sort of reaction from them. As you describe each picture, take the long string and wrap it around the heart a few times and then tie it onto the heart. As you add each picture, the heart will get more and more crowded with pictures and the string.)

Now, look at this heart. It has a lot of really cool things on it, but its' pretty crowded. There isn't much room left for other things. There isn't much room left for God, is there? He should be the very biggest, most important thing on our hearts, and if we let it get too clogged up with all our STUFF, there's no room left for Him. It's okay to have nice things and to like fun toys and

Polka Dot Girls ❀ Who Am I?

week 7

clothes, but we have to make sure that our hearts are God's alone – and that all our stuff isn't taking up too much room in our hearts. We need to love the LORD with all our hearts… not love our STUFF with all our hearts.

(*As you say this, begin removing all the pictures and string until you can see the words GOD again.*)

There's a story in the Bible about a man whose heart was all tied up in his STUFF instead of God. He was a very rich and important man, and one day He came to Jesus and asked Him what he should do in order to be one of His followers. Jesus asked him a couple of questions, and then finally He said to him, "*Then there's only one thing left to do: Sell everything you own and give it away to the poor. You will have riches in heaven. Then come, follow me." This was the last thing the official expected to hear. He was very rich and became terribly sad. He was holding on tight to a lot of things and not about to let them go.*" (Luke 18:22-23 MSG)

Why do you think Jesus asked the man to sell everything he had? Did Jesus want him to not have ANY money? No, I don't think so. I think Jesus knew that this man's heart was all tied up in his STUFF and so He asked him to give it all up. Unfortunately, this man wouldn't let go of all the things he had. He loved his STUFF more than he loved God.

So, how can we make sure that our hearts aren't too tied up with our stuff?

⇨ 1. Be content with your STUFF.

Do you know what the word "content" means? It means being happy with the way things are. Someone who is content isn't worried about getting more things, they are okay with what they have. Being content means you don't spend a lot of time thinking about what you don't have or what you want to by.

Jessica was OBSESSED with clothes. She just loved getting new things to wear. She would spend time on the computer looking at new outfits and she was always paying attention to the latest fashions. The problem was the more she looked at all the new stuff she wanted to get, the more she started to HATE

everything in her closet! All her clothes looked boring and old. She started to realize that her obsession with new clothes was making her not be content with the clothes she had.

Hebrews 13:5 says, *"Don't be obsessed with getting more material things. Be relaxed with what you have."* (MSG) God doesn't want you constantly thinking of all the STUFF you want to get. He wants you thinking about way more important things! When you start spending so much time thinking and asking for things, your heart gets more and more tied up in your stuff. Instead, God wants you to be thankful for the things you have! He wants you to have a grateful heart that is okay with the toys and clothes you have, thankful for things that you DO get and not always worrying about what you DON'T have.

The second way you can make sure your hearts aren't tied up with too much stuff is:

➡ 2. Know that you are SO much more than your STUFF.

Sometimes we can feel like we have to have just the right clothes or just the right toys in order for people to want to be our friends. When we don't feel confident about ourselves, it's easy to feel like a new shirt or a new toy will make us more comfortable or likeable.

But you don't need that stuff! God made you amazing and beautiful and fun, and you can be confident in who He made you to be. And if people only want to be your friend because of the things you have – then they're not really your friends anyway!

When you start to feel like you want to show off something new to make people like you better, stop yourself. When you feel like you need to have a new outfit so you won't feel nervous on the first day of school, remind yourself that God is with you and there is no need to be nervous! When you start relying on the things you have to make yourself feel better, take a minute and ask God to help you feel strong in Him and not in other things. Psalm 138:3 says, *As soon as I pray, you answer me; you encourage me by giving me strength.* God is all you need. You don't need all that stuff!

Polka Dot Girls ❀ Who Am I?

➡ 3. Don't worry about STUFF.

It can be easy to think about all the stuff we want, but there are times in our lives when our thoughts about money and things are way bigger than just wanting more stuff. For some of you, you are really worried about just having enough. Maybe your Mom and Dad are going through a hard time and your family just doesn't have much money at all. Maybe you want new things, but you know that your family can't afford them and so you feel kind of sad about that. Maybe you get teased at school because you don't have the same kind of clothes the other kids have.

Just because you're a kid doesn't mean you won't feel nervous and scared about money. It can be a really yucky feeling to be worried about having enough food or clothes. And feeling different from everyone because you can't afford certain clothes and toys is no fun at all.

But you know what? Jesus knew that you might feel worried about those things and He wrote some things in the Bible just for YOU! One of my favorite promises from God is found in Matthew 6:31-33. It says, *"So don't worry about these things, saying, 'What will we eat? What will we drink? What will we wear?' These things dominate the thoughts of unbelievers, but your heavenly Father already knows all your needs. Seek the Kingdom of God above all else, and live righteously, and he will give you everything you need."*

God has made you a promise. God promises that He will always take care of you. You don't need to worry about food and clothes, God will always provide for you. When you feel yourself starting to worry about these things, remind yourself that God will always take care of you. Always.

God cares so much for you. He loves to bless you with things. But He first and foremost wants you to love Him with all your heart. God wants you to love Him more than your STUFF.

> *Not that I was ever in need, for I have learned how to be content with whatever I have. I know how to live on almost nothing or with everything. I have learned the secret of living in every situation, whether it is with a full stomach or empty, with plenty or little. For I can do everything through Christ,[a] who gives me strength.* – Philippians 4:11-13

week 7

Kindergarten and 1st Grade Group Discussion Questions

1. Have you ever felt bad because you wanted something but couldn't have it?

2. Have you ever felt embarrassed because you didn't have a certain kind of clothes or a certain toy or game that all your friends have?

3. Practice saying today's theme verse together: *"For where your treasure is, there your heart will be also."* Matthew 6:21 (NIV)

4. What do you think that verse means?

    a. The things that we spend the most time and energy thinking about are the things closest to our hearts.

    b. Our hearts belong to the things we treasure most

    c. Our hearts are tied up with the things we are most concerned about.

5. Why is it so important to not have our STUFF be our treasure?

    a. Because God wants to have our hearts

    b. We shouldn't let anything in our hearts be more important to us than God is.

6. Why do you think Jesus asked the rich man to sell everything that he had?

    a. Because Jesus wanted to see if he loved his stuff more than he loved God.

    b. Jesus knew that this man was too concerned about his money

7. What does the word content mean?

    a. It means being happy with the way things are.

    b. Someone who is content isn't worried about getting more things, they are ok with what they have.

    c. Being content means you don't spend a lot of time thinking about what you don't have or what you want to by.

8. What are some ways that we can start to rely on our stuff to feel good about ourselves?

   a. By feeling like we need a new toy or outfit to make people to like us.

   b. Wanting to have new things so we can fit in with our friends

   c. Thinking that we're only as good as the clothes we have or the toys we have.

9. Do you ever worry about money? Is there something you want to share with the group? Take a minute and pray for the concerns the girls have.

week 7

2nd and 3rd Grade Group Discussion Questions

1. Have you ever felt bad because you wanted something but couldn't have it?

2. Have you ever felt embarrassed because you didn't have a certain kind of clothes or a certain toy or game that all your friends have?

3. Practice saying today's theme verse together: *"For where your treasure is, there your heart will be also."* Matthew 6:21 (NIV)

4. What do you think that verse means?

    a. The things that we spend the most time and energy thinking about are the things closest to our hearts.

    b. Our hearts belong to the things we treasure most

    c. Our hearts are tied up with the things we are most concerned about.

5. Why is it so important to not have our STUFF be our treasure?

    a. Because God wants to have our hearts

    b. We shouldn't let anything in our hearts be more important to us than God is.

6. Why do you think Jesus asked the rich man to sell everything that he had?

    a. Because Jesus wanted to see if he loved his stuff more than he loved God.

    b. Jesus knew that this man was too concerned about his money

7. What does the word content mean?

    a. It means being happy with the way things are.

    b. Someone who is content isn't worried about getting more things, they are ok with what they have.

    c. Being content means you don't spend a lot of time thinking about what you don't have or what you want to by.

8. Hebrews 13:5 says, *"Don't be **obsessed** with getting more material things. Be **relaxed** with what you have."* (MSG)

What are some ways we can obsess about our stuff?

   a. Always thinking about the new things you want to have

   b. Spending a lot of time asking for stuff

   c. Being selfish with your things and not sharing them with your friends or family.

9. What are some ways that we can start to rely on our stuff to feel good about ourselves?

   a. By feeling like we need a new toy or outfit to make people to like us.

   b. Wanting to have new things so we can fit in with our friends

   c. Thinking that we're only as good as the clothes we have or the toys we have.

10. Do you ever worry about money? Is there something you want to share with the group? Take a minute and pray for the concerns the girls have.

Polka Dot Girls ❁ Who Am I?

week 7

4th and 5th Grade Group Discussion Questions

1. Have you ever felt bad because you wanted something but couldn't have it?

2. Have you ever felt embarrassed because you didn't have a certain kind of clothes or a certain toy or game that all your friends have?

3. Practice saying today's theme verse together: *"For where your treasure is, there your heart will be also."* Matthew 6:21 (NIV)

4. What do you think that verse means?

    a. The things that we spend the most time and energy thinking about are the things closest to our hearts.

    b. Our hearts belong to the things we treasure most

    c. Our hearts are tied up with the things we are most concerned about.

5. Why is it so important to not have our STUFF be our treasure?

    a. Because God wants to have our hearts

    b. We shouldn't let anything in our hearts be more important to us than God is.

6. Why do you think Jesus asked the rich man to sell everything that he had?

    a. Because Jesus wanted to see if he loved his stuff more than he loved God.

    b. Jesus knew that this man was too concerned about his money

7. What does the word content mean?

    a. It means being happy with the way things are.

    b. Someone who is content isn't worried about getting more things, they are ok with what they have.

    c. Being content means you don't spend a lot of time thinking about what you don't have or what you want to by.

8. Hebrews 13:5 says, *"Don't be **obsessed** with getting more material things. Be **relaxed** with what you have."* (MSG)

    What are some ways we can obsess about our stuff?

    a. Always thinking about the new things you want to have

    b. Spending a lot of time asking for stuff

    c. Being selfish with your things and not sharing them with your friends or family.

9. What are some ways that we can start to rely on our stuff to feel good about ourselves?

    a. By feeling like we need a new toy or outfit to make people to like us.

    b. Wanting to have new things so we can fit in with our friends

    c. Thinking that we're only as good as the clothes we have or the toys we have.

10. Do you ever worry about money? Is there something you want to share with the group? Take a minute and pray for the concerns the girls have.

week 7

God Has MY Heart Necklace

Leaders: Make sure you do adequate preparation for the crafts in accordance to the age and skill level of your group. To expedite the process you may want to have the holes punched out of the hearts, as well as have the ribbon cut. For the younger girls you may want to thread and knot the ribbon as well.

Supplies Needed:

- Heart Shaped Foam
- Ribbon (approx. ¼" width)
- Plastic pony beads
- Hole Punch
- Scissors
- Glue
- Glitter
- Black Marker fine tip
- Smaller foam heart shapes (optional)
- Self-adhesive jewels (optional)

Prep:

- With a hole punch, make two holes at the outer corners of each side of the heart (Picture a clock in your mind's eye and put the holes at 11 and 1)
- Cut two pieces of ribbon approximately 12-18" each. The length may vary by girl.

What should we do?

- Thread one piece of ribbon through the first hole.
- Leave enough length to tie a knot in the front of the heart.
- Thread the other piece of ribbon through the second hole.

- Again…leave enough length to tie a knot in the front of the heart.
- Pull the ribbon tight so the knots rest on the heart.
- Add pony beads to each side of the ribbon.
- On the front or back of the heart write **Matthew 6:21**.
- Decorate the front of the heart with jewels and/or glitter.
- Tie the two pieces of ribbon around the girl's neck.
- The heart is a reminder to store your treasures in heaven and not in stuff!

Polka Dot Plus

week 7

Weekly Challenge

Grow: Grow by reading the story of the rich young ruler in **Luke 18:18-23**.

Love: Thank your Mom and Dad for all the things they give you. Tell them you appreciate all their hard work!

Act: Help combat your need for **STUFF** by giving something away to a friend or maybe even your brother or sister!

Memorize: *"For where your treasure is, there your heart will be also."* – Matthew 6:21 (NIV)

Parent Partner

Well, Mom and Dad, I'm sure you are not shocked to hear that our children struggle with materialism. Much like you and I can get wrapped up in our stuff, our girls can fall into the same trap. Our society continues to entice us with the newest and best thing and the compounded pressure of peer acceptance can infect our girls with a huge case of the "Gotta Have It's."

The number one thing you can do to help your daughter have a healthy attitude about money and things, is to have your own healthy attitude about money and things. Do a quick inventory of your own heart. Are you content with what you have? Are you demonstrating a level of gratefulness? Are you trusting God with your finances, or are you full of worry and anxiety?

Our children need to see us model healthy views about stuff. I constantly catch myself talking about "what I want" or "what I want to buy" and have to continually remind myself that little eyes are watching and little ears are listening. I am striving to live my life the way Hebrews 13:5 tells me to. *"Don't be obsessed with getting more material things. Be relaxed with what you have."* (MSG)

And lastly, trust that God will take care of your family. When we commit to honoring God with our money, we can trust that He will provide for us. In these times where finances can be of great concern, we can boldly know that God has promised to always take care of us. What greater legacy to leave our children than one of unquenchable faith in God our provider.

week 7

Kindergarten and 1st Grade
Take Home Activity Sheet

Deuteronomy 6:5 says that we are to *"Love the Lord your God with all your heart."* That means that we are to love GOD more than anything else. That our hearts belong to HIM alone.

Color and decorate the heart. As you color remind yourself that He should be the very biggest, most important thing on our hearts!

Polka Dot Girls ❦ Who Am I?

week 7

2nd and 3rd Grade Take Home Activity Sheet

Read the scripture the below. Circle the best answer. Go to your Bible and check your answers! All scriptures NIV.

1. *For where your treasure is, there your _____ will be also.* – Matthew 6:21

    a. dog   b. God   c. heart

2. *Love the Lord your God with all your _____.* – Deuteronomy 6:5

    a. strength   b. heart   c. mind

3. *Keep your lives free from the love of money and be _____ with what you have.* – Hebrews 13:5

    a. happy   b. content   c. ok

4. *³¹So do not _____, saying, 'What shall we eat?' or 'What shall we drink?' or 'What shall we wear?' ³²For the pagans run after all these things, and your heavenly Father knows that you need them. ³³But seek first his kingdom and his righteousness, and all these things will be given to you as well.* – Matthew 6:31-33

    a. pout   b. ask God   c. worry

5. *¹²I know what it is to be in need, and I know what it is to have plenty. I have learned the secret of being content in any and every situation, whether well fed or hungry, whether living in plenty or in want. ¹³I can do _____ this through him who gives me strength.* – Philippians 4:12-13

    a. nothing   b. all   c. most things

6. *Watch out! Be on your guard against all kinds of _____; a man's life does not consist in the abundance of his possessions.* – Luke 12:15

    a. greed   b. evil   c. money

7. *Set your minds on things above, not on _____ things.*
   – Colossians 3:2

      a. material   b. earthly   c. human

8. *And God is able to bless you abundantly, so that in all things at all times, having all that you _____, you will abound in every good work.*
   – 2 Corinthians 9:8

      a. want   b. desire   c. need

week 7

4th and 5th Grade Take Home Activity Sheet

- Read the scripture the below.
- Find the missing word from the list
- Go to your Bible and check your answers! All scripture NIV.

1. *For where your treasure is, there your _____ will be also.*
   – Matthew 6:21

2. *Keep your lives free from the love of money and be _____ with what you have.* – Hebrews 13:5

3. *³¹So do not _____, saying, 'What shall we eat?' or 'What shall we drink?' or 'What shall we wear?' ³²For the pagans run after all these things, and your heavenly Father knows that you need them. ³³But seek first his kingdom and his righteousness, and all these things will be given to you as well.* – Matthew 6:31-33

4. *Love the Lord your God with all your _____.*
   – Deuteronomy 6:5

5. *¹²I know what it is to be in need, and I know what it is to have plenty. I have learned the secret of being content in any and every situation, whether well fed or hungry, whether living in plenty or in want. ¹³I can do _____ this through him who gives me strength.* – Philippians 4:12-13

6. *Watch out! Be on your guard against all kinds of _____; a man's life does not consist in the abundance of his possessions.* – Luke 12:15

7. *Set your minds on things above, not on _____ things.*
   – Colossians 3:2

8. *And God is able to bless you abundantly, so that in all things at all times, having all that you _____, you will abound in every good work.*
   – 2 Corinthians 9:8

Word list:

| content | worry | need | all |
| heart | greed | earthly | heart |

Who Am I?

week 8

Courage

WHAT'S THE POINT?

GOD GIVES ME COURAGE TO FACE TOUGH SITUATIONS, TAKE A STAND AGAINST WRONG WORDS OR ACTIONS AND HELPS ME DO THINGS BIGGER THAN I CAN EVER IMAGINE.

theme verse

Be strong and courageous! Do not be afraid or discouraged. For the Lord your God is with you wherever you go.
Joshua 1:9

related bible story

Deuteronomy 31:1-8

❊ Large Group Lesson ❊

I am scared to death of grasshoppers. Yup… grasshoppers. I know that seems like a silly thing to be scared of, but I just can't seem to help it! They are so weird looking and they jump up on you out of nowhere. Ick! One time I came inside after working in my yard and my daughter said to me, "Mom, there's something on your back." Just then this H-U-G-E grasshopper jumped off my back right onto the kitchen counter. I screamed and jumped and screamed and ran around in circles and then screamed a little more until it finally jumped into the sink and washed down the drain. My kids still tease me about that all the time.

There are silly little things that we are all scared of (like grasshoppers) but there are lots of other REALLY scary things that you and I have to face every day. Maybe you are super scared of walking into a classroom where you don't know anybody. Maybe you're afraid of having to be away from your mom and dad. Maybe you're scared of the dark or of getting lost.

Being scared is no fun. Some people want to cry when they're scared. Other people get angry when they're scared. Sometimes it can make your tummy feel really strange. Some kids want to hide behind their mom or dad and some of us just don't know WHAT to do!

Fear can keep us from trying new things and from meeting new people. It can make us too scared to dream big dreams and live the life God has planned for us. And that is why God talks a lot about the way to fight fear… by having courage.

Courage is being able to do something even though you are scared. Courage is standing strong when everything in you wants to run and hide. Courage is doing the right thing even when the wrong thing seems easier. Courage fights fear.

God wants you to be courageous. He wants you to face your fears and stand strong. The Bible is full of stories that talk about people overcoming things that they were really, really afraid of. In each one of those stories, God helped the person get past their fears and go on to do really amazing things.

One of those stories was about a guy named Joshua. When God led the children of Israel out of Egypt, Moses was the leader chosen to guide the people. And one of his helpers was Joshua.

When Moses was 120 years old (yikes!) he stood in front of the people and made a speech. He said, *"I am now 120 years old, and I am no longer able to lead you. The Lord has told me, 'You will not cross the Jordan River.' But the Lord God yourself will cross over ahead of you. He will destroy the nations living there , and you will take possession of the land. Joshua will lead you across the river, just as the Lord promise."* (Deuteronomy 31:2-3)

week 8

Uhm... what?!? Can you imagine what Joshua must have been thinking in that moment? Me?! I am going to lead the people now... into a land of people that want to kill us?!? Can you imagine how scared he must have been? Not only did he have to take over for... you know... MOSES – like the greatest leader ever, he had to lead the people into a new land that had all kinds of people that hated them. Not the easiest job!!

I'm sure that in that moment Joshua felt a LOT of things – but more than anything I bet Joshua felt SCARED. I bet his stomach got all tied up in knots and his hands started to shake. I bet his mind started listing all the reasons there was NO WAY he could do the job. I bet he was FULL of fear.

But then Moses says something very important to Joshua. *"Then Moses called for Joshua, and as all Israel watched, he said to him, 'Be strong and courageous! For you will lead these people into the land that the Lord swore to their ancestors he would give them... Do not be afraid or discouraged, for the Lord will personally go ahead of you. He will be with you; he will neither fail you or abandon you.'"* (Deuteronomy 31:7-8)

Isn't that cool! It's like God knew exactly how Joshua would be feeling in that moment and He had Moses speak these words to help Joshua fight his fear. God knew that Joshua would be scared. He knew that he would feel overwhelmed. He knew that he would doubt his abilities.

But God made a promise to Joshua in that moment. He told him that He would be with him. He said that He would never fail or abandon him. God tells Joshua to stand and be courageous because HE was going to be always be with him.

And God makes the exact same promise to you and I. You don't have to be afraid of ANYTHING because God will always be with you and help you. He will never fail you. He will never leave you.

So, what are some ways that you can be COURAGEOUS? How can you fight fear and get past some of the things that you're scared of?

Well, first of all, you must

➡ 1. Be Brave!

What does it mean to be brave? Well, being brave means that when you feel afraid to do something, instead of quitting or running away from the thing you're afraid of, you do it anyway.

Emma was going through a hard time. She was afraid of being away from her mom and dad. For some reason, she just didn't want to go to friend's houses anymore or sleepover at her Grandma's. Whenever she would start to go somewhere without her parents, she would get this horrible feeling and she would get so nervous that she just stayed home.

Her mom and dad prayed with her that God would help her overcome her fear. She even began to memorize the scripture Psalm 118:6, *"The Lord is for me, so I will have no fear."* She knew that God would be with her whenever she went somewhere, even if her mom and dad weren't with her.

And so, one day a friend asked if she would like to come over to her house for a play date. At first, she felt the old familiar scary feeling, and she was ready to just stay home. But then, she realized that she needed to fight her fear and be brave. So, even though she felt a little nervous, she took a deep breath and went over to her friend's house. And once she got there, she had SO much fun! She was so glad that she didn't let her fear stop her from spending time with her friend.

The next time a friend asked her to come over, she was still a little afraid, but it was easier that time. Again, she took a deep breath, reminded herself that God was always with her, and decided to be brave. After a few times, she didn't even feel scared any more!

Sometimes we have to do things even though we're a little nervous. Sometimes we have to be brave and face our fears. Maybe you have been afraid of the dark and you need to ask God to help you be brave. Maybe you have been afraid of talking to a person you want to be friends with, and God is asking you to take a deep breath and talk to them – even if you're nervous. Being brave means you don't let your fear stop you from doing something. And Jesus will **ALWAYS** help you to be brave.

Polka Dot Girls ❋ Who Am I?

week 8

Another way you can learn to be courageous is to

➡ 2. Stand Up!

Have you ever been in a situation where someone was saying or doing something that you knew was wrong? Have you ever been around someone who was telling you to do something that you didn't want to do, but you felt really nervous about saying no? Have you ever had a friend treating you badly, but you were too scared to stick up for yourself?

Sometimes the best way we can show courage is by standing up. Sometimes we have to stand up to people who are doing something wrong and tell them to stop. Sometimes we have to speak up and say "no," even if it means that person might make fun of us or not want to be our friend anymore. And sometimes, we have to stand up to someone who is treating us poorly and tell them to stop.

Shannon was in a tough situation. Her friend Stephanie hadn't studied for her math test and during lunch, she leaned over and asked Shannon if she could copy her answers during the test. Shannon knew that it was wrong and she REALLY didn't want to cheat, but she was scared of what Stephanie would say or do if she didn't help her. At firsts, she nodded her head okay, but the moment she did that, in her heart she knew that it wasn't the right thing.

Everything in her was super scared to stand up to Stephanie. But she knew that it was the right thing to do. So, she mustered up all the courage she could and said, "I'm sorry, Stephanie, but I just can't do that. I wouldn't feel right about that." Stephanie gave her a snotty look and walked away angry. Shannon definitely didn't feel good about the fact that Stephanie was mad at her, but she knew in her heart that she had made the right decision. It took a lot of courage to stand up to her, but she was so thankful that she did.

Whenever you have to face another person and you are nervous about standing up to them, remember this verse. Hebrews 13:6 says, *"So we can say with confidence, 'the Lord is my helper, so I will have no fear. What can mere people do to me?'"* Remember that people are just people! It's way more important to do the right thing even if it means that someone might be mad at you for a while. God is with you and will give you the courage to stand up for what it right.

And the last way you can learn to be courageous is to

➡ 3. Take a Chance!

McKenzie had a dream. She loved to dance and she dreamed about being a ballet dancer when she grew up. Her teacher was always encouraging her and she practiced hard every day. Then one day her teacher told her that she thought she should transfer to another ballet school, one that was for more advanced dancers.

McKenzie was thankful for the opportunity, but she was also terrified of going to a new school where she didn't know anyone at all. In addition to that, her new teachers were going to be much harder on her and push her more than the teacher she had now. Everything about it made her excited, and everything about it made her nervous.

What should she do? Stay where she was and not have to face the fear of trying something new? Or take a chance and see just how far she could go. She knew that the new school wouldn't be easy, but it would help her live her dream.

After praying about it, she decided to go for it. She knew that God would be with her and that He would help her face anything difficult. No matter what, she could count on the fact that God would be with her. And the more she thought about it, maybe God wanted to use her to share His love with the girls and teachers at her new school. Not only could she learn more about dance, but she could be a light to those who didn't know Him. No matter how scared she was, she knew that helping God show His love to the world was something she wanted to do.

God will put big dreams in your heart. BIG dreams. And sometimes those dreams can seem way bigger than anything you could ever do on your own. Some people look at the size of their dreams and just get scared and discouraged and give up. They let their fear keep them from trying something new.

But God wants to help you do big things for Him! Ephesians 3:20 says, *"God can do anything, you know—far more than you could ever imagine or guess or request in your wildest dreams!"* (MSG) God wants to use you to do things bigger than you can even imagine!

Polka Dot Girls ❀ Who Am I?

And sometimes that is going to feel pretty scary. And if you let your fear keep you from stepping into what God has for you, you're going to miss out on some really great stuff. But if you fight your fear and look to God to give you courage, you will do great things!

We all have things that we're scared of. But we don't have to let our fear keep us from doing things, standing up for ourselves, and dreaming big. With God on our side, we have nothing to fear.

Closing Prayer: God, I am thankful that you go ahead of me and are always with me in whatever I do. Knowing that helps me to be courageous. Amen

Be Brave! Stand Up! Take a Chance!

Polka Dot Girls ❦ Who Am I?

week 8

Kindergarten and 1st Grade Group Discussion Questions

1. What is something that you are afraid of?

2. What is courage?

    a. Courage is being able to do something even though you are scared.

    b. Courage is standing strong when everything in you wants to run and hide.

    c. Courage is doing the right thing even when the wrong thing seems easier.

    d. Courage fights fear.

3. What promise does God make to Joshua when he became the leader of the children of Israel?

    a. God promised Joshua that He would be with him.

    b. He said that He would never fail or abandon him.

    c. God tells Joshua to stand and be courageous because HE was going to be always be with him.

4. What does it mean to be brave?

    a. Being brave means that when you feel afraid to do something, instead of quitting or running away from the thing you're afraid of, you do it anyway.

5. Have you ever been scared of something and then done it anyway? Share your story with the group.

6. Have you ever had to stand up to someone who wanted you to do something wrong or was mistreating you?

7. What are some of the dreams that God has put in your heart? Share one thing with the group.

Polka Dot Girls ❀ Who Am I?

week 8

2nd and 3rd Grade Group Discussion Questions

1. What is something that you are afraid of?

2. What is courage?

   a. Courage is being able to do something even though you are scared.

   b. Courage is standing strong when everything in you wants to run and hide.

   c. Courage is doing the right thing even when the wrong thing seems easier.

   d. Courage fights fear.

3. What promise does God make to Joshua when he became the leader of the children of Israel?

   a. God promised Joshua that He would be with him.

   b. He said that He would never fail or abandon him.

   c. God tells Joshua to stand and be courageous because HE was going to be always be with him.

4. What does it mean to be brave?

   a. Being brave means that when you feel afraid to do something, instead of quitting or running away from the thing you're afraid of, you do it anyway.

5. Have you ever been scared of something and then done it anyway? Share your story with the group.

6. Have you ever had to stand up to someone who wanted you to do something wrong or was mistreating you?

7. What are some of the dreams that God has put in your heart? Share one thing with the group.

Polka Dot Girls ♣ Who Am I?

week 8

4th and 5th Grade Group Discussion Questions

1. What is something that you are afraid of?

2. What is courage?

   a. Courage is being able to do something even though you are scared.

   b. Courage is standing strong when everything in you wants to run and hide.

   c. Courage is doing the right thing even when the wrong thing seems easier.

   d. Courage fights fear.

3. What promise does God make to Joshua when he became the leader of the children of Israel?

   a. God promised Joshua that He would be with him.

   b. He said that He would never fail or abandon him.

   c. God tells Joshua to stand and be courageous because HE was going to be always be with him.

4. What does it mean to be brave?

   a. Being brave means that when you feel afraid to do something, instead of quitting or running away from the thing you're afraid of, you do it anyway.

5. Have you ever been scared of something and then done it anyway? Share your story with the group.

6. Have you ever had to stand up to someone who wanted you to do something wrong or was mistreating you?

7. What are some of the dreams that God has put in your heart? Share one thing with the group.

week 8

God's Coupon Book

Supplies Needed:

- Colored cardstock for coupon cover
- White cardstock for coupons
- Markers/Crayons
- Pretty embellishments
- Stapler

Prep:

- Copy the template of God's Coupon Book cover onto your favorite color cardstock.
- Cut out each coupon cover.
- Copy the coupon templates on white cardstock

What should we do?

- Give each girl a copy of the coupon cover.
- Give each girl a copy of the coupon templates.
- Cut out the coupons.
- Decorate the coupon cover and coupons with markers/crayons and/or pretty embellishments.
- Complete the coupons with your goals on bravery, standing up for what is right and your dreams.
- Staple the cover and coupons together on the left side to create a booklet.

Templates:

1. Cover: God's Coupon Book
2. Inside: Coupons below

 # God's COUPON BOOK

 # God's COUPON BOOK

 # God's COUPON BOOK

Good for unlimited amounts of
BRAVERY!

What _____

When _____

The Lord is for me, so I will have no fear. – Psalm 118:6

Good for unlimited amounts of
Self-Confidence
to stand up for what is right!

To Who or For What _____

When _____

So we can say with confidence, "The Lord is my helper, so I will have no fear. What can mere people do to me?" – Hebrews 13:6

Good for unlimited amounts of
COURAGE
to accomplish your wildest dreams!

What _____

When _____

God can do anything, you know – far more than you could ever imagine or guess or request in your wildest dreams! – Ephesians 3:20 MSG

Polka Dot Girls ❖ Who Am I?

Polka Dot Plus

week 8

Weekly Challenge

Grow: Grow by reading the story of Joshua in **Joshua 1:1-9**.

Love: If you see someone struggling with fear (maybe a friend or your brother or sister) remind then that God will give them courage!

Act: Next time you feel afraid of something, take a deep breath and face the fear head on. Ask God for courage and then just go for it!

Memorize: *"Be strong and courageous! Do not be afraid or discouraged. For the Lord your God is with you wherever you go."* – Joshua 1:9

Parent Partner

I have watched all of my children struggle with varied levels of fear in their lives. Each of them have battled seasons of homesickness, fear of trying new things, and even fear of the dark. (and spiders… don't even get me started on the spiders.)

In all my motherly wisdom, I rarely know what to say in those moments. Even the most irrational fears are so very real to them. My best efforts at talking them out of their fears have remained fruitless.

BUT. I have seen their fears subside when I teach them to bring their fears to God. Reminding them that He is always with them seems to comfort them and help them through it. I have learned to give them the incredible gift of knowing that God is with them and that He will help them to be brave.

This week's lesson challenged the girls to be courageous in three ways:

- First of all, we encouraged them to be brave by facing their fears. Instead of giving in to the fear, we talked about fighting fear with bravery.

- Secondly, we discussed being courageous by standing up. Standing up for what's right, standing up when people want you to do something that is wrong, and standing up to people who aren't treating you the way you should be treated.

- And lastly, we told the girls to demonstrate bravery by taking a chance. God has big plans for their lives and in order to step into everything He has for them, they are going to need to try some things that seem far beyond what they think they can do. But God is always faithful and if they trust and rely on Him, He will help them to accomplish above and beyond anything they could imagine. They simply need to trust Him enough to take a chance—even when they are afraid.

Polka Dot Girls ❀ Who Am I?

week 8

Kindergarten and 1st Grade
Take Home Activity Sheet

In the space provided, draw a picture of how you can show courage.

You don't have to be afraid of ANYTHING because God will always be with you and help you. He will never fail you. He will never leave you.

The verses below talk about having courage. Read each verse and write the word COURAGEOUS in the blank spaces.

So be strong and _____! Do not be afraid and do not panic before them. For the Lord your God will personally go ahead of you. He will neither fail you nor abandon you. – Deuteronomy 31:6

This is my command—be strong and _____! Do not be afraid or discouraged. For the Lord your God is with you wherever you go. – Joshua 1:9

Be on guard. Stand firm in the faith. Be _____. Be strong. – 1 Corinthians 16:13

Being brave means you DON'T let your fear stop you from doing something. And Jesus will ALWAYS help you to be brave. Read each verse and write the word FEAR in the blank spaces.

So we can say with confidence, "The Lord is my helper, so I will have NO _____. What can mere people do to me?" – Hebrews 13:6

Yes, you came when I called; you told me, "Do NOT _____."
– Lamentations 3:57

For God has NOT given us a spirit of _____ and timidity, but of power, love, and self-discipline. – 2 Timothy 1:7

Polka Dot Girls ❧ Who Am I?

week 8

2nd and 3rd Grade Take Home Activity Sheet

You don't have to be afraid of ANYTHING because God will always be with you and help you. He will never fail you. He will never leave you.

Cross out the Js, Qs, Ls and Ps to find a message from God about courage!

P Q B L J E J J P O L Q N J J Q G P Q L J U Q L J J A Q Q P R L P L D .
P P Q J J S Q P L L J T Q L L A P J P N Q L Q J D P L P L F J I P P R Q J Q Q M P
Q L I L L N Q L P Q T J H L L E J L J J F P J L A Q I P P J T Q H .
L P B Q E J J C O Q L U J R L L A P J Q G Q L L E J O P P U J L S .
P P L B Q E J S P P T Q R J L O Q N J J L P G .
1 J C L O P P R Q J I L L N P T L Q H L J I P P A Q L N P S : P Q 1 L J 6 : Q 1 P 3

Line 1 _____

Line 2 _____

Line 3 _____

Line 4 _____

Line 5 _____

Line 6 _____

Being brave means you DON'T let your fear stop you from doing something. And Jesus will ALWAYS help you to be brave. Read each verse and write the word FEAR in the blank spaces.

So we can say with confidence, "The Lord is my helper, so I will have NO _____. What can mere people do to me?" – Hebrews 13:6

*Yes, you came when I called; you told me, "Do **NOT** _____."*
– Lamentations 3:57

*For God has **NOT** given us a spirit of _____ and timidity, but of power, love, and self-discipline.* – 2 Timothy 1:7

Polka Dot Girls ❖ Who Am I?

week 8

4th and 5th Grade Take Home Activity Sheet

You don't have to be afraid of ANYTHING because God will always be with you and help you. He will never fail you. He will never leave you.

Unscramble the bolded letters, to make the words, to find a message from God about courage!

Be **orngst** ___ ___ ___ ___ ___ ___ *and*

eruocusoag ___ ___ ___ ___ ___ ___ ___ ___ ___ .

Do not be **fdriaa** ___ ___ ___ ___ ___ ___ *or terrified*

because of **mhte** ___ ___ ___ ___ ,

for the **rLdo** ___ ___ ___ ___ *your God*

goes with **oyu** ___ ___ ___ ;

odG ___ ___ ___ *will personally go*

he will never **avlee** ___ ___ ___ ___ ___

nor **ekafsro** ___ ___ ___ ___ ___ ___ ___ *you.*

ouermDnyteo ___ ___ ___ ___ ___ ___ ___ ___ ___ ___ ___ 31:6 NIV

And Jesus will ALWAYS help you to be brave. Read each verse and write the word FEAR in the blank spaces.

So we can say with confidence, "The Lord is my helper, so I will have **NO** _____ . *What can mere people do to me?"* – Hebrews 13:6

*Yes, you came when I called; you told me, "Do **NOT** _____."*
– Lamentations 3:57

*For God has **NOT** given us a spirit of _____ and timidity, but of power, love, and self-discipline.* – 2 Timothy 1:7

Polka Dot Party

Poka Dot Party is a night for your girls to connect, invite their friends, and have FUN! Put together an exciting, special event for the girls to simply enjoy each other, do some fun activities, and tell their friends how FUN Polka Dot Girls is! This is a great way to give the girls something exciting to look forward to and when they're excited about something – they tell their friends! Really encourage them to bring a friend from school or their neighborhood with them.

There is no "lesson" for this night, because we simply want the girls to connect. I promise you, if their friends have an amazing night – they will want to come back! This is a great way to introduce the girls in your community to your church and leaders. Make sure your event is AWESOME!

At the end of the evening, be sure to send invited friends a promotional piece about your ministry. This is a great way to invite them back for the weekend with their parents!

Polka Dot Party
Theme: Spa Night

Food: You could provide "spa food" like veggies and fruits, but the girls would probably revolt. I suggest something fun like an ice cream sundae bar or root beer floats!

Games/Activities: Have various spa stations set up for the girls to visit.

1. Nail station where women or teenagers from your church can paint the girls nails. Invest in some fun colors and even little stickers to put on the girls nails!

2. Hair station where girls can get fun ponytails and up-dos. Buy combs (a new comb for each girl), bobby pins, small elastic bands and lots of color and glitter hairspray. Recruit the women in your church who do hair (or even just have 'girl hair experience' to run the hair station.)

3. Tattoo station where the girls can get a variety of fun sparkly temporary tattoos!

4. You could even have a massage station where the girls get fun shoulder rubs… who doesn't love that!?

Polka Dot Party
SPA NIGHT

Polka Dot Party
SPA NIGHT

Polka Dot Party Spa Night!

Come for a fun night to hang out with the girls! Get your hair and nails done and enjoy some fun snacks! Don't forget to invite a friend!

Where _____

When _____

Polka Dot Party Spa Night!

Come for a fun night to hang out with the girls! Get your hair and nails done and enjoy some fun snacks! Don't forget to invite a friend!

Where _____

When _____

www.ingramcontent.com/pod-product-compliance
Lightning Source LLC
Chambersburg PA
CBHW060512300426
44112CB00017B/2636